Just the Basics

of English Grammar

A workbook for the most common grammar and writing problems

By Sheldon Lawrence, Ph.D.

Sheldon Lawrence, Ph.D. ©2014

www.stillwaterspress.com
stillwaterspress@gmail.com

Table of Contents

Introduction: Effective and ineffective writing

Unfortunately, good writing is not a matter of learning a set of rules and then following those rules meticulously. Writing is art, and all of the great writers have occasionally broken the rules of grammar and punctuation in order to achieve a desired effect. The rules and tips in this book will only make sense as you develop an "ear" for good writing. When experienced writers sit down to write, they do not have a list of rules in their head, and then go about constructing sentences according to those rules. Instead, they know how good writing "sounds." Through a lifetime of reading, they have developed an intuitive sense of what sounds right and what doesn't sound right. The rules can help during revision to strengthen clarity and make easier reading, but knowing rules alone does not make a good writer.

Having said that, the rules of grammar, punctuation, style, and usage are often the things by which readers will judge you. You may have original and insightful things to say, but your meaning will be lost if your sentences are riddled with errors, awkward phrasing, misplaced punctuation, and incorrectly used words.

This book will help you strengthen the clarity of your ideas by helping you improve the grammar, punctuation, and style of your prose. Sometimes this is accomplished through choosing and arranging the right words. Sometimes it's accomplished by using punctuation to separate "chunks" of thought. And sometimes it's about digging deeper to find out what you really want to say. Most often, all three of these components work together as you write and revise your work.

There are a dizzying number of books about grammar, style, and editing. In my years of teaching writing, the concepts covered in this text represent those that most often plague student writing. This text does not go into great detail about the various exceptions and disagreements in the study of grammar. If you desire such detail, you have many good books to choose from. If you want just the basics, then this workbook will give you the tools you need to improve your grammar and style in the most straightforward way possible.

Meet the Sentence

Parts of speech

Sometimes grammar books throw around a lot of fancy terms, but in reality, sentences are pretty simple things. Think of a sentence as a cake. It only takes a few simple ingredients to make a cake—flour, sugar, eggs, water. But you can also add all sorts of things to the cake to make it more interesting and delicious.

A sentence only needs two basic ingredients: a noun and a verb.

> Dogs run.

Dogs is a noun. *Run* is a verb.

Everything else tacked onto the sentence just adds information and detail.

> Dogs run around whenever they are let off of their leashes.

In this section, we'll briefly review the ingredients of a sentence; these are referred to as the "parts of speech." Some parts of speech are essential to building sentences; these are the nouns (or pronouns) and verbs. Others are like frosting and decorations on a cake—they aren't absolutely essential to create a sentence, but they add information, flavor, and character.

Verbs

The most basic ingredient in the sentence is a verb. Action verbs indicate what is happening or being done. There are hundreds of different action verbs.

> Action verb: George **eats** candy.

Another kind of verb, called a linking verb, functions like an equals sign.

> Linking verb: George **seems** nice. (George = nice)

"Be" verbs also act as linking verbs by leveling out the sentence like an equal sign. There are only eight be verbs: be, being, been, was, were, is, am, are.

> Be verb: George **is** quiet. (George = quiet)

Nouns

Nouns indicate people, places, things, ideas, and emotions.

> carpenter, officer, lake, tree, boat, democracy, anger, happiness

Nouns that refer to specific things are called proper nouns.

> Jennifer, Yellowstone, Lake Tahoe, Titanic, Microsoft

Pronouns

Pronouns can replace nouns to avoid the awkward repetition of the same noun. Here is a sentence without pronouns.

> I like my car when my car has just been washed because my car's bright red paint shines in the sun.

Now read the sentence with pronouns.

> I like my car when it has just been washed because its bright red paint shines in the sun.

The pronoun "it" stands in for "car" to make the sentence less tiresome.

Common Pronouns

You don't need to worry about the terminology, but read through the lists below to get a sense of the different types of pronouns and how they could replace some other noun.

> **Personal pronouns:** I, me, my, mine, you, your, yours, he, she, it, him, her, his, its, we, us, our, ours, you, your, yours, they, them, their, theirs.

> **Demonstrative pronouns:** this, that, these, those

> **Relative pronouns:** who, whom, whose, which, that

> **Indefinite pronouns:** another, anybody, anything, everyone, nobody, someone, both, many, any, most, some

Adjectives

Adjectives are words that describe or "modify" nouns and pronouns. If someone says a car has been modified, you know it has been enhanced or dressed up. In relation to nouns, adjectives usually describe "which one," "how many," or "what kind."

warm coat   **red** car   **silly** person   **obnoxious** child   **seven** cookies

Adverbs

Adverbs are kind of like adjectives in that they modify or describe another word, but they modify verbs, adjectives, and other adverbs. Adverbs answer the following questions:

How? He ate **slowly**.

When? We will eat **soon**.

Where? I want to eat **here**.

How often? Let's eat **frequently**.

To what extent? We will eat **enough**.

Prepositions

Prepositions describe the "position" or relationship between words and ideas in a sentence. Review the following list of common prepositions and notice how most indicate position in time or space.

about	despite	out
above	down	over
across	during	past
after	except	since
along	for	through
among	from	to
around	in	toward
at	inside	under
before	into	until
below	of	up
beside	off	with
between	on	within
by	onto	without

Prepositions are always followed by nouns. This combination is called a prepositional phrase.

among the trees   **into** the car   **during** my lunch break   **from** my grandmother

Conjunctions

Conjunctions join (or "conjoin") words or parts of a sentence. Two important types of conjunctions are **coordinating conjunctions** and **subordinating conjunctions**.

The coordinating conjunctions are **for, and, nor, but, or, yet, so**. (Use the word **fanboys** to remember these conjunctions.)

I hate snowboarding, **but** I love skiing.

I have not seen the movie, **so** you are ruining it for me.

Note: The word "for" can act as both a preposition and a coordinating conjunction. It is a conjunction when it means "because" or "since" and a preposition all other times. The use of "for" as a conjunction is somewhat archaic.

Conjunction: She left her coat, for it was very hot outside.

Preposition: I waited in the lobby for two hours.

There are many subordinating conjunctions; the following list provides a few of the most common.

after	even though	unless
although	if	until
as	once	when
as long as	since	whenever
because	than	wherever
before	that	while

Notice how these words can join two parts of a sentence.

I cannot go swimming **because** I just ate a huge meal.

People had to look up information in the library **before** the internet was developed.

When a sentence begins with a subordinating conjunction, a comma is used where the first clause ends (see "Building a Sentence").

Because I just ate a huge meal, I cannot go swimming.

Before the internet was developed, people had to look up information in a library.

Interjections

Interjections express surprise, concern, or other strong emotions. They stand alone or usually come at the beginning of sentences. Interjections should not be used much, if at all, in formal writing. Common interjections are hey, wow, ouch, well, great, oh, yeah, whoa.

Hey, get over here.

Great! The plans are coming together.

Well, I guess that's the way it goes.

Meet the Sentence–Exercise A

Underline the verbs in the following sentences.

1. George loves baseball and plays it every day.

2. His team lost the game last week, but George maintains a good attitude.

3. He believes that whenever he loses, he learns a different lesson.

4. Because he has such a good attitude, he is never a sore loser, unlike some of his teammates who only play to win.

Meet the Sentence–Exercise B

Underline the nouns in the following sentences.

1. The cafeteria lunch is never very good at the local school.

2. Mary is trying to make a petition so the school board will change the food.

3. She wants there to be a menu with many options, such as salads, pasta, grilled meat, and fruits.

4. Students usually agree with Mary, but some want more desserts, such as cheesecake, ice cream, and pie.

Meet the Sentence–Exercise C

Underline the pronouns in the following sentences.

1. Finding good study habits is hard for me because I am so easily distracted.

2. It is even harder to study because I have a roommate who plays his drums all day long.

3. Any time I start doing my work, he will suddenly start pounding away at them.

4. This is not going to work for me, but I am too shy to tell him to stop.

Meet the Sentence–Exercise D

Underline the adjectives in the following sentences.

1. The first day we went to Yellowstone was beautiful and sunny.

2. We saw a huge buffalo resting on the dusty ground and a brown bear grazing on a distant mountain.

3. On our way home, inky black clouds gathered in the sky, and rumbling thunder shook our car.

4. I didn't know that such a peaceful day could turn so ugly and frightening.

Meet the Sentence–Exercise E

Underline the adverbs in the following sentences.

1. There is a creek that lazily winds its way behind my parent's house.

2. It is home to many snails that stubbornly latch on to the slimy rocks.

3. Whenever I walk down the creek, I usually try to avoid the snails by carefully stepping around them.

4. But there are so many of them that, regrettably, I sometimes crush a few.

Meet the Sentence–Exercise F

Underline the prepositions in the following sentences.

1. Last week, my friends and I decided to get tickets for a movie premiere before they were all sold out.

2. Despite the long line, we got our tickets, and last night we went to the midnight premiere.

3. We got to the theater two hours before the movie started since we wanted to get good seats.

4. During the movie, I fell asleep, but it wasn't that great anyway.

Meet the Sentence–Exercise G

Underline the conjunctions in the following sentences.

1. The library in my neighborhood has great librarians, but it is very small.

2. Even though they have limited funds, they always hold fun events for the community.

3. Because the events always introduce me to great books, I always try to go and bring my family.

4. If the library receives more funds, they'll be able to expand their collection, so I try to donate whenever I have a little extra cash.

Meet the Sentence–Exercise H

Underline the interjections in the following sentences.

1. Hey, Stacie.

2. Wow! You look nice.

3. Well, are you ready for our date?

4. Oh, I didn't realize you were thinking of this as a date.

Answer Key: Meet the Sentence–Exercise A

1. George <u>loves</u> baseball and <u>plays</u> it every day

2. His team <u>lost</u> the game last week, but George <u>maintains</u> a good attitude.

3. He <u>believes</u> that whenever he <u>loses</u>, he <u>learns</u> a different lesson.

4. Because he <u>has</u> such a good attitude, he <u>is</u> never a sore loser, unlike some of his teammates who only <u>play</u> to win.

Answer Key: Meet the Sentence–Exercise B

1. The cafeteria <u>lunch</u> is never very good at the local <u>school</u>.

2. <u>Mary</u> is trying to make a <u>petition</u> so the school <u>board</u> will change the <u>food</u>.

3. She wants there to be a <u>menu</u> with many <u>options</u>, such as <u>salads</u>, <u>pasta</u>, grilled <u>meat</u>, and <u>fruits</u>.

4. <u>Students</u> usually agree with <u>Mary</u>, but some want more <u>desserts</u>, such as <u>cheesecake</u>, <u>ice cream</u>, and <u>pie</u>.

Answer Key: Meet the Sentence–Exercise C

1. Finding good study habits is hard for <u>me</u> because <u>I</u> am so easily distracted.

2. <u>It</u> is even harder to study because <u>I</u> have a roommate <u>who</u> plays <u>his</u> drums all day long.

3. Any time <u>I</u> start doing my work, <u>he</u> will suddenly start pounding away at <u>them</u>.

4. <u>This</u> is not going to work for <u>me</u>, but <u>I</u> am too shy to tell <u>him</u> to stop.

Answer Key: Meet the Sentence–Exercise D

1. The <u>first</u> day we went to Yellowstone was <u>beautiful</u> and <u>sunny</u>.

2. We saw a <u>huge</u> buffalo resting on the <u>dusty</u> ground and a <u>brown</u> bear grazing on a <u>distant</u> mountain.

3. On our way home, <u>inky black</u> clouds gathered in the sky, and <u>rumbling</u> thunder shook our car.

4. I didn't know that such a <u>peaceful</u> day could turn so <u>ugly</u> and <u>frightening</u>.

Answer Key: Meet the Sentence–Exercise E

1. There is a creek that <u>lazily</u> winds its way behind my parent's house.

2. It is home to many snails that <u>stubbornly</u> latch on to the slimy rocks.

3. Whenever I walk down the creek, I <u>usually</u> try to avoid the snails by <u>carefully</u> stepping around them.

4. But there are so many of them that, <u>regrettably</u>, I <u>sometimes</u> crush a few.

Answer Key: Meet the Sentence–Exercise F

1. Last week, my friends and I decided to get tickets <u>for</u> a movie premiere <u>before</u> they were all sold out.

2. <u>Despite</u> the long line, we got our tickets, and last night we went <u>to</u> the midnight premiere.

3. We got <u>to</u> the theater two hours <u>before</u> the movie started since we wanted to get good seats.

4. <u>During</u> the movie, I fell asleep, but it wasn't that great anyway.

Answer Key: Meet the Sentence–Exercise G

1. The library in my neighborhood has great librarians, <u>but</u> it is very small.

2. <u>Even though</u> they have limited funds, they always hold fun events for the community.

3. <u>Because</u> the events always introduce me to great books, I try to go <u>and</u> bring my family.

4. <u>If</u> the library receives more funds, they'll be able to expand their collection, <u>so</u> I try to donate <u>whenever</u> I have a little extra cash.

Answer Key: Meet the Sentence–Exercise H

1. <u>Hey</u>, Stacie.

2. <u>Wow</u>! You look nice.

3. <u>Well</u>, are you ready for our date?

4. <u>Oh</u>, I didn't realize you were thinking of this as a date.

Building a Sentence

As stated in the previous chapter, a sentence only requires a verb, and then a noun or pronoun to "do" the action of the verb. Nouns or pronouns that function in this capacity are called the subject of the sentence.

>   Dogs eat.

This is a complete sentence. It has a subject, a verb, and it expresses a complete thought. This simple subject + verb construction forms the core of all sentences. Anything we tack on is just a nice addition.

Let's add a little more information. What do dogs eat?

>   Dogs eat **hamburgers**.

We just added another noun that tells us what dogs eat. This is called the object of the sentence. Where the subject is the "doer" of the verb, the object is the "receiver" of that action.

Let's say something about what kind of dogs. In other words, let's add an adjective.

>   The **skinny** dogs eat hamburgers.

Now, let's say something about how the dogs eat the hamburgers. In other words, let's describe or modify the verb with an adverb.

>   The skinny dogs eat hamburgers **slowly**.

Where does this eating happen? We can add a prepositional phrase that locates this sentence in time or space.

>   The skinny dogs eat hamburgers slowly **at the table**.

Imagine the next sentence in this line of thought looking like this:

>   Their owners don't seem to mind.

These two sentences can stand alone as complete thoughts. A group of words that contain a subject and a verb and express a complete thought is called an *independent clause*. We can let these independent clauses stand alone as sentences, or we can also choose to combine them with a conjunction. A *coordinating* conjunction would put the two sentences in a kind of equal relationship.

> The skinny dogs eat hamburgers slowly at the table, **and** their owners don't seem to mind.

If we added a *subordinating* conjunction, the second sentence would become subordinate or dependent on the first.

> The skinny dogs eat hamburgers slowly at the table **because** their owners don't seem to mind.

The second sentence would then be called a dependent clause, while the first one is still an independent clause.

Sentences will often begin with the dependent clause and put the independent clause on the end. When this occurs, a comma is placed at the end of the dependent clause.

> **Because their owners don't seem to mind**, the skinny dogs eat hamburgers slowly at the table.

Just for fun, let's keep building this sentence to make it increasingly complex. We'll use the construction with the coordinating conjunction and add another dependent clause with a subordinating conjunction.

> The skinny dogs eat hamburgers slowly at the table, **and** their owners don't seem to mind **as long as** they use good manners.

What we have here are basically three different clauses strung together. Each clause contains a subject and a verb. The conjunctions that join these clauses indicate their relationship to one another.

> The skinny dogs eat hamburgers slowly at the table.
>
> Their owners don't seem to mind.
>
> They use good manners.

A phrase is a group of related words that lack a subject, a verb, or both. Phrases can never stand alone as complete sentences. Remember that "at the table" is a prepositional phrase. Let's tack on a follow-up phrase to this sentence separated by a comma.

> The skinny dogs eat hamburgers slowly at the table, and their owners don't seem to mind as long as they use good manners, **especially when dining with guests.**

Let's add information about the owners. We'll interrupt the flow of the sentence by inserting the owner's names. Because this information interrupts the sentence, it will require commas.

> The skinny dogs eat hamburgers slowly at the table, and their owners, Pat and John, don't seem to mind as long as they use good manners, especially when dining with guests.

We can add more information about the guests.

> The skinny dogs eat hamburgers slowly at the table, and their owners, Pat and John, don't seem to mind as long as they use good manners, especially when dining with guests **visiting from foreign countries where things like dogs eating at tables is considered unusual and even impolite.**

The new information about the guests actually contains additional clauses, phrases, and adjectives. We can also experiment with different constructions to see what works best.

> Using good manners so as not to offend guests from foreign countries, Pat and John's skinny dogs eat hamburgers slowly at the table, a practice Pat and John don't seem to mind.

The point of this exercise is to demonstrate how a simple noun and a verb can serve as the foundation for complex sentences just by adding additional clauses, conjunctions, phrases, adjectives, adverbs, etc. Of course, you don't want to get carried away with simply adding stuff to a sentence. Short and simple sentences belong in good writing just as much as complex ones.

Building a Sentence–Exercise A

Using the "dogs eat" example as a model, practice starting with a simple clause (subject + verb) to create an increasingly complex sentence using the steps below. (Remember that in real writing, not all sentences must contain all the parts of speech or combine clauses. This is just an exercise to introduce you to the basics of sentence-building.)

1. Choose an interesting verb.

2. Choose a noun or pronoun to become the subject of that verb.

3. Add an "object" to the sentence to receive the action of the verb.

4. Add an adjective or adverb in an appropriate place.

5. Add a prepositional phrase.

6. Using a coordinating or subordinating conjunction, combine your sentence with another clause.

7. "Play" with your new sentence by using different conjunctions, adding phrases or clauses, or rearranging words.

Building a Sentence–Exercise B

Follow the directions given for each sentence below to make the sentences more interesting.

1. Combine the following sentences with a conjunction:
   I drove carefully to the concert. I still dented my dad's car.

2. Add adjectives to this sentence to make it more descriptive:
   I walked across the bridge and saw a forest filled with flowers and deer.

3. Combine the following sentences using a subordinating conjunction:
   My favorite dessert is cheesecake. It can be difficult to make.

4. Add adverbs to this sentence to make it more descriptive:
   The fall leaves drifted down the stream.

5. Add a prepositional phrase to this sentence:
   The pirates fought savagely.

Answer Key: Building a Sentence–Exercise A

Answers may vary.

An ugly cockroach sneakily approaches me, and all I can do is hide behind the door.

Answer Key: Building a Sentence–Exercise B

Answers may vary.

1. I drove carefully to the concert, but I still dented my dad's car.

2. I walked across the bridge and saw an enchanted forest filled with fragrant flowers and grazing deer.

3. My favorite dessert is cheesecake although it can be difficult to make.

4. The fall leaves drifted gracefully down the stream.

5. The pirates fought savagely on the deck of their ship.

Fragments

Fragments are not real sentences because they lack a subject, a verb, or a complete thought.

> Fragment: All day on the beach. (There is no **subject**, **verb**, or **complete thought** here. It leaves us asking, "What happened on the beach?" "Who did it?")

> Sentence: **We played** all day on the beach. (Here there is a **subject** [we], **verb** [played], and complete thought.)

Some kinds of fragments may contain a subject and a verb, but still need more information to be a complete thought.

> Fragment: As Jake was eating ice cream. (We have a subject [Jake] and a verb [was eating], but we are left waiting for more information because of the word "as.")

> Sentence: As Jake was eating ice cream, **he saw his ex-girlfriend**. (Now we have all three components of a sentence, so the statement makes complete sense.)

Identifying and Correcting Fragments

Fragments do not easily stand out when read with other sentences. Notice how the fragment in the following example seems to hide because it fits so nicely with the surrounding sentences.

> Anorexia, a growing problem among teens, is a type of eating disorder. Where people starve themselves for fear of becoming overweight. Learning about this problem is the first step in preventing it.

Identify fragments by looking at each sentence individually, and ask if it makes sense on its own.

1. Anorexia, a growing problem among teens, is a type of eating disorder.

2. Where people starve themselves for fear of becoming overweight.

3. Learning about this problem is the first step in preventing it.

Notice how the second "sentence" does not form a complete thought because of the word "where."

The most common way to fix a fragment is to combine it with the sentence that comes before or after.

Anorexia, a growing problem among teens, is a type of eating disorder where people starve themselves for fear of becoming overweight.

Another way to identify fragments is to apply the "random person" test. If you were to go up to a random person and state the supposed "sentence" alone, would you have said something complete and self-contained? Would the person completely understand you? Let's say we are suspicious of the following "sentences" and want to see if one is a fragment:

I eat a lot of chocolate. Whenever I am nervous or bored.

Imagine going up to a random person and saying, "I eat a lot of chocolate." Does that make sense? Has something complete been communicated? Yes, it makes sense standing alone. Now imagine you go up and say, "Whenever I am nervous or bored." Have you uttered a complete thought? Could the random person make sense of what you just said? No. This is a fragment. Again, this fragment is fixed by simply combining it with the previous sentence.

I eat a lot of chocolate whenever I am nervous or bored.

Note: When you apply this test, remember that pronouns can sometimes make it seem like a thought is not complete. For example: "It eats it." This is a complete sentence because it contains a subject, verb, and expresses a complete thought. Out of context, we don't know what "it" is, but **a pronoun functions as a subject** because it is replacing a noun.

Common Problem Areas

Fragments are really just "chunks" of sentences that have broken off from the main sentence. A few types of sentences seem to tempt writers to make fragments.

Introductory phrases

Fragment: Walking past the house. The mailman noticed the dog was off its leash.

Corrected: Walking past the house, the mailman noticed the dog was off its leash.

"Add-on" phrases (Phrases tagged on to the end of a sentence that require a comma, not a period)

> Fragment: I love reading good books. Especially when I am not assigned to read them.

> Corrected: I love reading good books**,** especially when I am not assigned to read them.

> Fragment: I felt like an outcast. Living on the edge of society.

> Corrected: I felt like an outcast, living on the edge of society.

Subordinating conjunctions (see "Building a Sentence")

> Fragment: Whenever I go back home. I hang out with my high school friends.

> Corrected: Whenever I go back home, I hang out with my high school friends.

> Fragment: I hang out with my friends from high school. Whenever I go back home.

> Corrected: I hang out with my friends from high school whenever I go back home. (Simply omit the period.)

> Fragment: Because I have never had good vision. I will never make a good pilot.

> Corrected: Because I have never had good vision, I will never make a good pilot.

Note: Sometimes fragments are intentional. Experienced writers will sometimes use fragments for stylistic purposes. You should avoid writing a fragment, however, unless you are certain of the particular effect you are trying to create by using it.

Fragments–Exercise A

Underline and correct the sentence fragments in the paragraph below.

> I love nature. I love its beauty and its peace. I grew up in a rural setting. Taking frequent trips to the nearby mountains. My childhood is filled with memories of family camping trips. Slow walks through groves of aspen and the sound of wind through pines. I love being where phones do not ring. Where car horns cannot be heard. Periodic immersion in the natural world offers a kind of spiritual renewal that cannot be found in the city. I don't mean to say that cities are bad. Just that it is nice to have a break from the city life every once in a while.

Fragments–Exercise B

Underline and correct the sentence fragments in the paragraph below.

My brothers are kind of crazy. They get together and watch what they call "epic lms" and eat strange snacks. Recently they watched *Lawrence of Arabia*. A movie with horses running, sand flying, and a weird white guy in a turban getting just a tad blood-thirsty. During intermission, my tallest brother busts out the cheese. I was worried it would be yucky, but it was white, soft, and delicately flavored. He produced a cracker. Smeared it with a light jalapeño jelly. Tucked the cheese into the jelly, and then balanced a chip of gourmet chocolate truffle on top. Last of all, an almond adorned the top. As strange as it sounds. It was actually quite delicious.

Fragments–Exercise C

Underline and correct the sentence fragments in the paragraph below.

I have to admit that I really hate sports. Now, don't get me wrong. No problem with athletes. I've met plenty of pleasant people who prefer sports. But if I attempt to be one of those muscled human beings. I inevitably end up splitting open my own head or someone else's. Between watching out for that hurtling ball, blocking my designated enemy, and avoiding the violence of absent-minded reflexes. It's all too much for me. Rather than flail my way through the next big game. I think I'll just go read a book.

Fragments–Exercise D

Underline and correct the sentence fragments in the paragraph below.

I didn't like doing chores as a child. I much preferred jamming to music or playing outside. Even in the cold Colorado winters. There was, however, one chore that I loved doing. So much that I would even take time out of my day to complete it. I shared the bathroom with three brothers, so over time, the mess would quickly accumulate. Boy's boxers littering the laundry hamper and toothpaste caked on the sink. At first I hated it, but I soon learned that a clean, sanitary environment was extremely satisfying. Plus, I could jam to music while I cleaned. Now I love cleaning the bathroom. Especially if it's just my own mess.

Answer Key: Fragments–Exercise A

Fragments are underlined. The second paragraph shows possible corrections.

I love nature. I love its beauty and its peace. I grew up in a rural setting. <u>Taking frequent trips to the nearby mountains.</u> My childhood is filled with memories of family camping trips. <u>Slow walks through groves of aspen and the sound of wind through pines.</u> I love being where phones do not ring. <u>Where car horns cannot be heard.</u> Periodic immersion in the natural world offers a kind of spiritual renewal that cannot be found in the city. I don't mean to say that cities are bad. <u>Just that it is nice to have a break from the city life every once in a while.</u>

Answers may vary.

I love nature. I love its beauty and its peace. I grew up in a rural setting, taking frequent trips to the nearby mountains. My childhood is filled with memories of family camping trips, slow walks through groves of aspen, and the sound of wind through pines. I love being where phones do not ring and where car horns cannot be heard. Periodic immersion in the natural world offers a kind of spiritual renewal that cannot be found in the city. I don't mean to say that cities are bad, just that it is nice to have a break from the city life every once in a while.

Answer Key: Fragments–Exercise B

Fragments are underlined. The second paragraph shows possible corrections.

My brothers are kind of crazy. They get together and watch what they call "epic lms" and eat strange snacks. Recently they watched *Lawrence of Arabia*. <u>A movie with horses running, sand flying, and a weird white guy in a turban getting just a tad blood-thirsty.</u> During intermission, my tallest brother busts out the cheese. I was worried it would be yucky, but it was white, soft, and delicately flavored. He produced a cracker. <u>Smeared it with a light jalapeño jelly. Tucked the cheese into the jelly, and then balanced a chip of gourmet chocolate truffle on top.</u> Last of all, an almond adorned the top. <u>As strange as it sounds.</u> It was actually quite delicious.

Answers may vary.

My brothers are kind of crazy. They get together and watch what they call "epic films" and eat strange snacks. Recently they watched *Lawrence of Arabia*, a movie with horses running, sand flying, and a weird white guy in a turban getting a bit too blood-thirsty. During intermission, my tallest brother busted out the cheese. I was worried it would be yucky, but it was white, soft, and delicately flavored. He produced a cracker, smeared it with a light jalapeño jelly, tucked the cheese into the jelly, and then balanced a chip of gourmet chocolate truffle on top. Last of all, an almond adorned the top. As strange as it sounds, it was actually quite delicious.

Answer Key: Fragments–Exercise C

Fragments are underlined. The second paragraph shows possible corrections.

I have to admit that I really hate sports. Now, don't get me wrong. <u>No problem with athletes.</u> I've met plenty of pleasant people who prefer sports. <u>But if I attempt to be one of those muscular human beings.</u> I inevitably end up splitting open my own head or someone else's. <u>Between watching out for that hurtling ball, blocking my designated enemy, and avoiding the violence of absent-minded reflexes.</u> It's all too much for me. <u>Rather than flail my way through the next big game.</u> I think I'll just go read a book.

Answers may vary.

I have to admit that I really hate sports. Now, don't get me wrong; I have no problem with athletes. I've met plenty of pleasant people who prefer sports. But if I attempt to be one of those muscular human beings, I inevitably end up splitting open my own head or someone else's. Watching out for that hurtling ball, blocking my designated enemy, and avoiding the violence of absent-minded reflexes are all too much for me. Rather than flail my way through the next big game, I think I'll just go read a book.

Answer Key: Fragments–Exercise D

Fragments are underlined. The second paragraph shows possible corrections.

I didn't like doing chores as a child. I much preferred jamming to music or playing outside. <u>Even in the cold Colorado winters.</u> There was, however, one chore that I loved doing. <u>So much that I would even take time out of my day to complete it.</u> I shared the bathroom with three brothers, so over time, the mess would quickly accumulate. <u>Boy's boxers littering the laundry hamper and toothpaste caked on the sink.</u> At first I hated it, but I soon learned that a clean, sanitary environment was extremely satisfying. Plus, I could jam to music while I cleaned. Now I love cleaning the bathroom. <u>Especially if it's just my own mess.</u>

Answers may vary.

> I didn't like doing chores as a child. I much preferred jamming to music or playing outside, even in the cold Colorado winters. There was, however, one chore that I loved doing so much that I would even take time out of my day to complete it. I shared the bathroom with three brothers, so over time, the mess would quickly accumulate. Boy's boxers littered the laundry hamper and toothpaste was caked on the sink. At first I hated it, but I soon learned that a clean, sanitary environment was extremely satisfying. Plus, I could jam to music while I cleaned. Now I love cleaning the bathroom, especially if it's just my own mess.

Run-on Sentences

A run-on results when two sentences (called "independent clauses") are joined without correct punctuation.

Comma Splice Run-ons

When two independent sentences are separated by a comma instead of a period, the result is called a comma splice.

Incorrect: Swimming is good exercise, I do it every morning.

Incorrect: I still haven't figured out Spanish, I've been studying it for years.

Incorrect: I have been waiting here for one hour, I'm going home.

Fix Option # 1: Join the independent clauses with coordinating conjunction (also called a FANBOYS conjunction: For, And, Nor, But, Or, Yet, So). A comma should be placed before the FANBOYS conjunction.

Correct: Swimming is good exercise, **so** I do it every morning.

Correct: I still haven't figured out Spanish, **and** I've been studying it for years.

Correct: I have been waiting here for one hour, **so** I'm going home.

Fix Option #2: Separate the sentences with a period.

Correct: Swimming is good exercise. I do it every morning.

Correct: I still haven't figured out Spanish. I've been studying it for years.

Correct: I have been waiting here for one hour. I'm going home.

Fix Option #3: Use a semicolon to separate the two sentences. A semicolon acts in the same way as a period in that it separates two complete sentences, but it indicates a close relationship between the sentences.

Correct: Swimming is good exercise; I do it every morning.

Correct: I still haven't figured out Spanish; I've been studying it for years.

Correct: I have been waiting here for one hour; I'm going home.

Fused Sentence Run-ons

Sometimes two independent sentences are run together without punctuation or a conjunction. These are called fused sentences. You can fix fused sentences using the same options described in the "comma splices" section above.

Incorrect: I hope to see a movie this weekend there is a new one in the dollar theater.

Fix Option #1: Add a conjunction to join the sentences. (In this example the conjunction does not need a comma because it is a subordinating conjunction.)

Correct: I hope to see a movie this weekend **because** there is a new one in the dollar theater.

Fix Option #2: Separate the sentences with a period.

Correct: I hope to see a movie this weekend**.** There is a new one in the dollar theater.

Fix Option #3: Use a semicolon to indicate a close relationship between the two sentences.

Correct: I hope to see a movie this weekend**;** there is a new one in the dollar theater.

Run-ons—Exercise A

Underline the group of words where the comma splice or fused sentence occurs. Once you have identified the run-ons, correct them.

They did it again why do people keep doing this? All I'm asking for is that my roommates show a little courtesy. Why can't they place the toilet paper roll on the correct way it's not that hard! You just take the toilet paper, unhinge the bar, and slip the roll on with the squares facing you. Why would anyone in their right mind place the squares on the wall side? It makes restroom breaks so stressful, you have to then awkwardly reach your hand up through the bar to grab the paper and then rip it off while making sure you don't unwind the whole roll. I swear if this happens again, I'm going to be the one unwound.

Run-ons—Exercise B

Underline the portion of the sentence where the comma splice or fused sentence occurs. Once you have identified the run-ons, correct them.

My ideal vacation involves going somewhere interesting, and then not doing much at all. I don't like busy vacations I don't want to feel like I have to take a vacation from my vacation. I like rest for example, I would love to visit Italy, but touring the famous sites wouldn't be my idea of fun. I would rather rent a little villa in the country or along the coast I would just live like a local for a few weeks. The Vatican, the Parthenon, and the Leaning Tower have been around for a while, they can wait a little longer for me to see them. Some may call it boring, I call it actually getting some much needed rest.

Run-ons—Exercise C

Underline the portion of the sentence where the comma splice or fused sentence occurs. Once you have identified the run-ons, correct them.

The Giving Tree by Shel Silverstein is more than just a children's book, it encompasses so much about how I want to live my life and raise my children. The themes of service, sacrifice, and simplicity can be incorporated into any part of my life, the tree serves this little boy his entire life and loves him with every branch and leaf it ever gave. In contrast, as the little boy grows and becomes more ambitious, he only finds discontentment. *The Giving Tree* shows why service and contentment with the simple things are such key aspects of being truly happy, that's why I read this book once a year.

Run-ons—Exercise D

Underline the portion of the sentence where the comma splice or fused sentence occurs. Once you have identified the run-ons, correct them.

Last week my boyfriend and I went ice-skating, it was a frigid night. When we left the house, we were shocked with freezing winds that chilled us to our bones. Upon arriving at the ice-skating rink, we had to switch out our shoes with ice-skating shoes normally this would be easy, but our frozen fingers had to claw at our shoelaces. After gleefully sliding around on the ice for half an hour, we both decided the cold was just too much, we needed to get inside to a warm place. After we got warmed up, we drank hot chocolate and watched a movie we should have just done that to begin with and skipped the skating.

Answer Key: Run-ons—Exercise A

Corrections are underlined. Answers may vary.

They did it <u>again. Why</u> do people keep doing this? All I'm asking for is that my roommates show a little courtesy. Why can't they place the toilet paper roll on the correct <u>way? It's</u> not that hard! You just take the toilet paper, unhinge the bar, and slip the roll on with the squares facing you. Why would anyone in their right mind place the squares on the wall side? It makes restroom breaks so <u>stressful because you</u> have to then awkwardly reach your hand up through the bar to grab the paper and then rip it off while making sure you don't unwind the whole roll. I swear if this happens again, I'm going to be the one unwound.

Answer Key: Run-ons—Exercise B

Corrections are underlined. Answers may vary.

My ideal vacation involves going somewhere interesting, and then not doing much at all. I don't like busy <u>vacations. I don't</u> want to feel like I have to take a vacation from my vacation. I like <u>rest. For</u> example, I would love to visit Italy, but touring the famous sites wouldn't be my idea of fun. I would rather rent a little villa in the country or along the <u>coast. I would</u> just live like a local for a few weeks.

The Vatican, the Parthenon, and the Leaning Tower have been around for a <u>while, so they</u> can wait a little longer for me to see them. Some may call it <u>boring; I call</u> it actually getting some much needed rest.

Answer Key: Run-ons—Exercise C

Corrections are underlined. Answers may vary.

The Giving Tree by Shel Silverstein is more than just a children's <u>book; it</u> encompasses so much about how I want to live my life and raise my children. The themes of service, sacrifice, and simplicity can be incorporated into any part of my <u>life. The</u> tree serves this little boy his entire life and loves him with every branch and leaf it ever gave. In contrast, as the little boy grows and becomes more ambitious, he only finds discontentment. *The Giving Tree* shows why service and contentment with the simple things are such key aspects of being truly <u>happy. That's</u> why I read this book once a year.

Answer Key: Run-ons—Exercise D

Corrections are underlined. Answers may vary.

Last week my boyfriend and I went <u>ice-skating. It</u> was a frigid night. When we left the house, we were shocked with freezing winds that chilled us to our bones. Upon arriving at the ice-skating rink, we had to switch out our shoes with ice-skating <u>shoes. Normally</u> this would be easy, but our frozen fingers had to claw at our shoelaces. After gleefully sliding around on the ice for half an hour, we both decided the cold was just too <u>much; we</u> needed to get inside to a warm place. After we got warmed up, we drank hot chocolate and watched a <u>movie. We</u> should have just done that to begin with and skipped the skating.

Commas

The explanations and exercises that follow will introduce you to the most common comma rules and help you develop an intuitive sense of how commas affect sentence rhythm and meaning. Not all comma rules are set in stone; writers can include or omit a comma if necessary to achieve a desired rhythm or avoid confusion. However, as with all stylistic choices, it is important to know the rules before knowing how and why to bend them.

FANBOYS: For, And, Nor, But, Or, Yet, So (coordinating conjunctions)

When two independent sentences (clauses) are joined by a FANBOYS conjunction, a comma should be placed before the conjunction.

> Incorrect: Some toy dolls promote unrealistic body images among young girls **yet** toy companies continue to market these products without restraint.

The conjunction here is "yet." Look at what comes before "yet." Is "Some toy dolls promote unrealistic body images among young girls" a complete sentence? Yes. Now look at what comes after "yet." Is "Toy companies continue to market these products without restraint" a complete sentence? Yes. Two independent sentences are joined by a FANBOYS conjunction; therefore, place a comma before "yet."

> Correct: Some toy dolls promote unrealistic body images among young girls, **yet** toy companies continue to market these products without restraint.

Here are a few more examples:

> Incorrect: Yesterday was my birthday but we are celebrating it this weekend.

> Correct: Yesterday was my birthday, but we are celebrating it this weekend.

> Incorrect: The resort offers tennis and golf for adults and the kids will enjoy the water park.

> Correct: The resort offers tennis and golf for adults, and the kids will enjoy the water park.

If what follows the conjunction cannot stand alone as a sentence (is not an independent clause), then no comma is necessary.

Correct: The resort offers tennis and golf for adults and a water park for kids.

If the two independent clauses joined by the conjunction are very short, then the comma can be omitted.

Acceptable: Dogs are forgiving and cats are indifferent.

Dependent Clauses

When a sentence begins with a dependent clause, use a comma to separate it from the independent clause (the rest of the sentence).

The words in the table (subordinating conjunctions) are common indicators of a dependent clause:

If	Whenever	Unless
When	Before	Until
Although	After	Whatever
As	Since	While

When subordinating conjunctions are in the middle of the sentence, they usually do not need a comma.

Correct: I will make you cookies _if_ you come over today.

When the sentence begins with a subordinating conjunction, there is a natural pause where the dependent clause ends and the independent clause begins. Read the sentence aloud and listen for the natural pause.

Example: **If you come over today,** I will make you cookies.

A comma is placed between the dependent clause and the independent clause.

Incorrect: When it is hot outside I like to eat ice cream.

Correct: When it is hot outside, I like to eat ice cream.

Try making up some sentences that begin with the words in the table. See if you can hear the natural pause between the clauses as you create the sentence.

Introductory Words and Phrases

Place a comma after a word or expression that introduces a sentence. These words usually indicate a transition or provide commentary on the sentence that follows. Here are some common introductory words.

Finally, the check arrived in the mail.

Unfortunately, it is not what you know but who you know.

Luckily, we won't be going through that whitewater again.

Of course, not everyone enjoys the sensation of jumping out of an airplane.

However, do not get too comfortable with your present situation.

In the end, doing a job imperfectly is better than never trying at all.

First, you should understand the costs involved in starting a business.

Second, you must decide whether you are willing to pay that price.

Next, draft a business plan and let someone review it for potential problems.

Also, don't forget to apply for a business license.

In contrast, those who study and pay attention in class usually do well on exams.

For example, one student who stopped text-messaging in class improved by one letter grade.

In the meantime, he was able to catch up on the meaningless conversations after class.

The above words only require a comma when they are functioning as introductory words. Sometimes they function as core parts of a sentence; in these cases, they will not require a comma. You must decide whether the word is functioning as an introductory word or as a core part of the sentence.

Next in line to be CEO is our former coworker Sally Brown. (not an introductory word)

Next, press the gas pedal to the floor and hold on for your life. (introductory word)

Of course I love you. (not an introductory expression)

Of course, not everyone needs to be given so much reassurance. (introductory expression)

Place a comma after a phrase that introduces or leads into the main part of a sentence. This rule applies in a way similar to the dependent clause rule.

> Kissing in the display window, the couple drew quite a crowd.

> Of all the candidates running for office, he was my least favorite.

> Wanting to make an impression, I rented a convertible for my first date.

> With that in mind, we can move forward with the proposal.

Follow-up Elements

Place a comma before a word or phrase at the end of a sentence that serves as an afterthought. Sometimes these afterthoughts are short follow-up questions.

> It is the first house on the left, I believe.

> I love getting gifts for Valentine's Day, don't you?

> The house was quiet, almost too quiet.

Items in a Series

Use a comma to separate three or more items in a series. These items can be single words or whole phrases.

> My high school buddies and I went to France, Spain, and Italy after we graduated.

> Tomorrow I need to wash my laundry, pay the bills, and buy some new shoes.

The most common error with lists is placing the comma before the first item in the list. It is correct to place the comma after the first item.

> Incorrect: I am looking for a partner who is, trustworthy, caring, and funny.

> Correct: I am looking for a partner who is trustworthy, caring, and funny.

Note: While it is more common to put a comma after the second-to-last item (before "and"), some writers and style guides choose to omit it. These exercises use the comma.

In a complex list, using only commas can cause confusion. Use a semicolon between pairs of words intended as a single unit but that could be misread as separate items.

Confusing: Last summer I travelled to New York, Paris, France, Rome, Italy and Moscow, Russia.

Better: Last summer I travelled to New York; Paris, France; Rome, Italy; and Moscow, Russia.

Nonessential Interrupting Words and Phrases

Place commas around a word or phrase that meets these two conditions:

1. The word or phrase is additional information and not necessary for the sentence to make sense.

2. The word or phrase interrupts the flow of the sentence, almost as if it could be put in parentheses.

We cannot, **however,** allow them to launch another attack.

This is the first time, **I believe,** we have been faced with layoffs.

You understand, **of course,** that pets require a lot of work.

Yellowstone, **the nation's first national park,** welcomes millions of visitors every year.

George Washington, **although an inspirational leader,** was not a brilliant military strategist.

Note: Sometimes names can be unnecessary information. Look at the example:

My mom, **Charlene,** took ballroom dancing for three years.

Because Charlene is surrounded in commas, we can assume that the author of this sentence has only one mom, and the author is simply pointing out her name, which is not necessary information. However, look at the following sentence:

My friend Jamey forgets her cell phone whenever she leaves the house.

Because there are no commas surrounding Jamey, we can assume that the author has many friends because the name, Jamey, is necessary to identify which friend the author is talking about. Be aware that this is not the same rule that is used with addressing someone directly as stated below.

Dates and Places

Place a comma between the city and state or nation.

> I grew up in Billings, Montana.

> They went on their honeymoon to Paris, France.

If in the middle or beginning of the sentence, a comma goes after the state or nation.

> I grew up in Billings, Montana, during the 1980s.

Place a comma between and after the date and the year.

> America declared independence from Britain on July 4, 1776.

> On July 4th, 1776, American colonies declared independence from Britain.

Note: Omit the comma if the sentence does not give the day of the month.

> June 1944 marked an important turning point in World War II.

> I was born in October of 1965.

Addressing Someone Directly

Place commas around a person or group directly addressed in the sentence. If the person is being referred to, but not addressed directly, no comma is needed.

> First of all, **Mandy,** you need to spend more time doing homework.

> **Sarah,** please accept my apology for forgetting about our date.

> I wonder if David will come to my party on Saturday. (David is being referred to, so no comma necessary).

Commas–Exercise A

In the sentences below, add necessary commas using the FANBOYS rule. Not all sentences will require a comma.

1. I like writing poetry occasionally but my real passion is writing short fiction.

2. Some people don't like reading fiction because they feel it is pointless to get

emotionally involved in a story that did not really happen.

3. Fictional stories are obviously not true yet they do contain what could be called emotional truth.

4. Novels, for example, are a way to explore universal emotions and experiences to which people can relate.

5. Many novelists will base their stories on their personal life or they will draw on the life of real historical figures.

6. Fiction writers don't always reveal whether their stories are based on real experience so you cannot say that novels are always purely fictional.

7. One type of novel is even called an "autobiographical novel" because it is so heavily based on the life of the author.

8. The category "nonfiction" can be misleading as well for not all autobiographies are as factual as the authors indicate.

9. Some memoirists have been accused of embellishing the facts and rearranging the sequencing of events to make their life story sound more interesting.

10. I'm not saying there is no difference between a true story and a fictional one but you can see that the line between fiction and nonfiction is not as sharp and distinct as many think.

Commas—Exercise B

In the sentences below, add necessary commas using the dependent clause rule. Not all sentences will require a comma.

1. Whenever I would drive to work on a particular road I had a feeling that I would get into a car crash there someday.

2. Although I had never been in a car wreck it seemed like I was overdue.

3. This point in my life was before I understood that our thoughts can create our reality.

4. As I was going to work one morning I noticed how the sun was just coming up over the horizon straight ahead of me.

5. I could barely see the road because the sun was so bright in my eyes.

6. When I approached the intersection I barely noticed traffic had stopped due to construction.

7. Although I was able to stop in time the person behind me was not so attentive.

8. I came to a complete stop when suddenly I heard screeching tires behind me.

9. Before I realized what was happening the car slammed into me going 40 miles per hour.

10. While both cars were completely wrecked nobody was badly hurt.

Commas—Exercise C

In the sentences below, add necessary commas using the introductory word or phrase rule. Not all sentences will require a comma.

1. Unfortunately going fishing with children is not always the charming activity people make it out to be.

2. The first difficulty is finding the right place.

3. Second you need to mentally prepare for the fact that you will not do any serious fishing on this trip.

4. Third tell your children that fishing is a relaxing sport that requires patience.

5. When you find a place with lots of easy-to-catch fish, bait the hook and cast it into the pond.

6. Next wait for about two minutes until your kids get bored.

7. Fighting the boredom your child will throw rocks into the water.

8. With all the patience you can muster you explain that this will scare away the fish.

9. In the meantime mosquitoes will make a feast of you and the child.

10. Luckily you have a plan B; pack up and head to the nearest swimming pool.

Commas—Exercise D

In the sentences below, add necessary commas using the follow-up elements rule. Not all sentences will require a comma.

1. That was the best restaurant we've been to don't you think?

2. It was even better than the one we went to in Paris if you can imagine.

3. The steak was cooked to perfection.

4. The chef was trained at a prestigious school I think.

5. The waiter was helpful but not overbearing or intrusive.

6. Everything was delicious especially the dessert.

7. I ordered dessert first because I was feeling rebellious.

8. I discovered that eating dessert first does not ruin your appetite not even a little.

9. Everything about this restaurant was perfect almost too perfect.

10. The experience was worth the high price wasn't it?

Commas—Exercise E

In the sentences below, add necessary commas using the items in a series rule. Not all sentences will require a comma.

1. Summer is a time when families make memories of good food and good times.

2. Taste buds are treated to things like watermelon barbeque and lemonade.

3. The sounds of summer include good music buzzing bees sprinklers and chirping crickets.

4. Even chores like mowing the lawn weeding the garden and washing the car can be fun in the summer.

5. Friends money and a little laziness are necessary ingredients for a good summer vacation.

6. When I was a kid, my parents ran a marina and boat rental business.

7. I remember working hard playing hard and getting into a little trouble.

8. After the boats were cleaned the shelves were stocked and the floors were swept, we would go water skiing.

9. At night, after the store was closed, we played video games and ate ice cream.

10. I hope people can make their own memories of fun adventure and good food.

Commas—Exercise F

In the sentences below, add necessary commas using the non-essential, interrupting phrases rule. (Make sure the phrase meets **both** criteria). Not all sentences will require a comma.

1. My favorite pastime what many consider to be a "guilty pleasure" is watching television.

2. I believe this activity is mostly a waste of time.

3. That fact however does not stop me from plopping in front of the couch after a hard day of work.

4. Cooking shows especially those featuring cooking contests are my favorite.

5. Watching all of that cooking of course makes me hungry.

6. Instead of cooking something like what I see on TV, I reach for the nearest junk food.

7. My cooking skills while not as good those of the chefs on TV are not all that bad.

8. The problem I believe is the expense involved in getting all the ingredients.

9. Watching TV and eating can if taken to extremes create bad health habits.

10. In my case however I am far too busy for these leisure activities to take over my life.

Commas—Exercise G

In the sentences below, add necessary commas using the dates and places rule. Not all sentences will require a comma.

1. President Kennedy was assassinated on November 22 1963 in Dallas Texas.

2. I'll meet you in San Francisco on October 23.

3. London England is one of the world's most important financial centers.

4. I will never forget the floods during April of 2006.

5. Next year I am traveling to New York, Chicago, and Paris France.

6. The Unites States entered World War II when Japan bombed Pearl Harbor Hawaii on December 7 1941.

7. If you travel to Southeast Asia during the rainy season, don't forget your umbrella.

8. Los Angeles California enjoys a mild climate throughout the year.

9. January 1st of 2000 marked the beginning of a new millennium.

10. The football schedule will be announced in June in Denver Colorado.

Commas—Exercise H

In the sentences below, add necessary commas using the direct address rule. Not all sentences will require a comma.

1. My friend Bob is a great guy.

2. I said, "Mom when is your birthday?"

3. Daniel I didn't get the email you sent about the work party.

4. When I saw Andy at the concert, I was surprised because he had called in sick.

5. You need to know Mr. President that this won't look good for the next elections.

6. The writer Charles Dickens was one of the most prolific authors of the Victorian period.

7. Sally why didn't you report that your purse was stolen?

8. The problem Son is that your grades have suffered since we bought the video game.

9. Give the book to Dave when you are finished.

10. When you get back to the United States, John will help you find a place to stay.

Commas—Exercise I

In the paragraph below, add necessary commas using all the rules in this chapter. Not all sentences will require a comma.

I grew up in New Haven Connecticut close enough to the shore that my family could go and visit the Saybrook Point Marina. We watched deep sea fishermen proudly display largemouth bass sharks and swordfish. To me it seemed the whole world smelled of fresh seawater. At the end of the day my parents would bring us to a fish house called Lenny and Joe's a well kept local secret. My parents would split a lobster and dip the meat in bowls of melted butter. My brothers would ask for steamed oysters and then they would slurp down necks and bellies like vacuums. Since I'm not a big fan of seafood I got the cheeseburger every time. One time my mom said to me "You know Sarah someday you will regret not taking advantage of this fresh seafood." My family told me I didn't belong in New England. Unfortunately I couldn't help it. I really hated the taste of fish.

Answer Key: Commas—Exercise A

1. I like writing poetry occasionally, but my real passion is writing short fiction.

2. Some people don't like reading fiction because they feel it is pointless to get emotionally involved in a story that did not really happen. **(no correction)**

3. Fictional stories are obviously not true, yet they do contain what could be called emotional truth.

4. Novels, for example, are a way to explore universal emotions and experiences to which people can relate. **(no correction)**

5. Many novelists will base their stories on their personal life, or they will draw on the life of real historical figures.

6. Fiction writers don't always reveal whether their stories are based on real experience, so you cannot say that novels are always purely fictional.

7. One type of novel is even called an "autobiographical novel" because it is so heavily based on the life of the author. **(no correction)**

8. The category "nonfiction" can be misleading as well, for not all autobiographies are as factual as the authors indicate.

9. Some memoirists have been accused of embellishing the facts and rearranging the sequencing of events to make their life story sound more interesting. **(no correction)**

10. I'm not saying there is no difference between a true story and a fictional one, but you can see that the line between fiction and nonfiction is not as sharp and distinct as many think.

Answer Key: Commas—Exercise B

1. Whenever I would drive to work on a particular road, I had a feeling that I would get into a car crash there someday.

2. Although I had never been in a car wreck, it seemed like I was overdue.

3. This point in my life was before I understood that our thoughts can create our reality. **(no correction)**

4. As I was going to work one morning, I noticed how the sun was just coming up over the horizon straight ahead of me.

5. I could barely see the road because the sun was so bright in my eyes. **(no correction)**

6. When I approached the intersection, I barely noticed traffic had stopped due to construction.

7. Although I was able to stop in time, the person behind me was not so attentive.

8. I came to a complete stop when suddenly I heard screeching tires behind me. **(no correction)**

9. Before I realized what was happening, the car slammed into me going 40 miles per hour.

10. While both cars were completely wrecked, nobody was badly hurt.

Answer Key: Commas—Exercise C

1. Unfortunately, going fishing with children is not always the charming activity people make it out to be.

2. The first difficulty is finding the right place. **(no correction)**

3. Second, you need to mentally prepare for the fact that you will not do any serious fishing on this trip.

4. Third, tell your children that fishing is a relaxing sport that requires patience.

5. When you find a place with lots of easy-to-catch fish, bait the hook and cast it into the pond. **(no correction)**

6. Next, wait for about two minutes until your kids get bored.

7. Fighting the boredom, your child will throw rocks into the water.

8. With all the patience you can muster, you explain that this will scare away the fish.

9. In the meantime, mosquitoes will make a feast of you and the child.

10. Luckily, you have a plan B; pack up and head to the nearest swimming pool.

Answer Key: Commas—Exercise D

1. That was the best restaurant we've been to, don't you think?

2. It was even better than the one we went to in Paris, if you can imagine.

3. The steak was cooked to perfection. **(no correction)**

4. The chef was trained at a prestigious school, I think.

5. The waiter was helpful but not overbearing or intrusive. **(no correction)**

6. Everything was delicious, especially the dessert.

7. I ordered dessert first because I was feeling rebellious. **(no correction)**

8. I discovered that eating dessert first does not ruin your appetite, not even a little.

9. Everything about this restaurant was perfect, almost too perfect.

10. The experience was worth the high price, wasn't it?

Answer Key: Commas—Exercise E

1. Summer is a time when families make memories of good food and good times. **(no correction)**

2. Taste buds are treated to things like watermelon, barbeque, and lemonade.

3. The sounds of summer include good music, buzzing bees, sprinklers, and chirping crickets.

4. Even chores like mowing the lawn, weeding the garden, and washing the car can be fun in the summer.

5. Friends, money, and a little laziness are necessary ingredients for a good summer vacation.

6. When I was a kid, my parents ran a marina and boat rental business. **(no correction)**

7. I remember working hard, playing hard, and getting into a little trouble.

8. After the boats were cleaned, the shelves were stocked, and the floors were swept, we would go water skiing.

9. At night, after the store was closed, we played video games and ate ice cream. **(no correction)**

10. I hope people can make their own memories of fun adventure and good food. **(no correction)**

Answer Key: Commas–Exercise F

1. My favorite pastime, what many consider to be a "guilty pleasure," is watching television.

2. I believe this activity is mostly a waste of time. **(no correction)**

3. That fact, however, does not stop me from plopping in front of the couch after a hard day of work.

4. Cooking shows, especially those featuring cooking contests, are my favorite.

5. Watching all of that cooking, of course, makes me hungry.

6. Instead of cooking something like what I see on TV, I reach for the nearest junk food. **(no correction)**

7. My cooking skills, while not as good those of the chefs on TV, are not all that bad.

8. The problem, I believe, is the expense involved in getting all the ingredients.

9. Watching TV and eating can, if taken to extremes, create bad health habits.

10. In my case, however, I am far too busy for these leisure activities to take over my life.

Answer Key: Commas—Exercise G

1. President Kennedy was assassinated on November 22, 1963, in Dallas, Texas.

2. I'll meet you in San Francisco on October 23. **(no correction)**

3. London, England, is one of the world's most important financial centers.

4. I will never forget the floods during April of 2006. **(no correction)**

5. Next year I am traveling to New York, Chicago, and Paris, France.

6. The Unites States entered World War II when Japan bombed Pearl Harbor, Hawaii, on December 7, 1941.

7. If you travel to Southeast Asia during the rainy season, don't forget your umbrella. **(no correction)**

8. Los Angeles, California, enjoys a mild climate throughout the year.

9. January 1st of 2000 marked the beginning of a new millennium. **(no correction)**

10. The football schedule will be announced in June in Denver, Colorado.

Answer Key: Commas—Exercise H

1. My friend Bob is a great guy. **(no correction)**

2. I said, "Mom, when is your birthday?"

3. Daniel, I didn't get the email you sent about the work party.

4. When I saw Andy at the concert, I was surprised because he had called in sick. **(no correction)**

5. You need to know, Mr. President, that this won't look good for the next elections.

6. The writer Charles Dickens was one of the most prolific authors of the Victorian period. **(no correction)**

7. Sally, why didn't you report that your purse was stolen?

8. The problem, Son, is that your grades have suffered since we bought the video game.

9. Give the book to Dave when you are finished. **(no correction)**

10. When you get back to the United States, John will help you find a place to stay. **(no correction)**

Answer Key: Commas—Exercise I

I grew up in New Haven, Connecticut, close enough to the shore that my family could go and visit the Saybrook Point Marina. We watched deep sea fishermen proudly display largemouth bass, sharks, and swordfish. To me it seemed the whole world smelled of fresh seawater. At the end of the day, my parents would bring us to a fish house called Lenny and Joe's, a well kept local secret. My parents would split a lobster and dip the meat in bowls of melted butter. My brothers would ask for steamed oysters, and then they would slurp down necks and bellies like vacuums. Since I'm not a big fan of seafood, I got the cheeseburger every time. One time my mom said to me, "You know, Sarah, someday you will regret not taking advantage of this fresh seafood." My family told me I didn't belong in New England. Unfortunately, I couldn't help it. I really hated the taste of fish.

Confused Words

Some words sound alike but have different meanings and different spellings. These words, called homophones, often create confusion in writing. While there are many such words, the following list represents a few of most common ones that give writers trouble.

accept/except

Accept is a verb. In other words, someone or something must be doing the accepting.

> I accept your proposal of marriage.

> That store does not accept credit cards.

Except functions like the word "excluding."

> I like all ice cream flavors except chocolate.

> I am free every day except Thursday.

Hint: If you want to exclude something, use except because they both start with exc. Accept is an action (verb), and both begin with A.

affect/effect

Affect is a verb; someone or something must "affect" something else.

> That movie affected me quite a bit. (The movie did the affecting.)

Effect mostly functions as a noun.

> That movie had an effect on my sleep. (Effect is a "thing" (noun) that happened as a result of the movie.)

Hint: Affect starts with an "A" like the word action, so that is the verb.

are/our

Are is a form of the verb "be" and describes a state of being or functions as an equals sign linking two parts of a sentence.

> We are driving to California next week.

Our is the possessive form of "we."

> We are driving to California next week. Our grandparents are meeting us there.

conscience/conscious

Conscience is your inner voice that tells you what is right or wrong.

> My conscience told me not to stay at that party.

Conscious indicates awareness.

> I felt self-conscious on my first day of class.

Hint: Your inner voice reminds you of the SCIENCE of right and wrong = conSCIENCE

farther/further

Farther refers to a distance that can be measured.

> How much farther do we have to walk?

Further indicates unmeasurable, abstract distance.

> I don't want to talk about this any further.

Hint: A = actual (fArther), U = unreal (fUrther)

feel/fill

Feel means to touch something or have a sensation.

> I feel happy when my friends come to visit me.

Fill means to make full.

> Please fill that vase with water.

its/it's

Its is the possessive form of the pronoun "it."

> The dog lost its collar while we were camping.

It's is the contraction for "it is."

> It's not too late to change your mind.

Hint: The source of confusion here is that we think an apostrophe is used to show possession (Bob's car). While this is true, the word "its" is already a possessive word by nature, like the words "his" or "her." You do not need to make it possessive with an apostrophe. Whenever you come across "it's" read it as "it is."

lay/lie

Lay is a verb and must be accompanied by an object.

> Lay the paper down on the desk.

Lie means "to recline."

> You should go lie down on the bed.

Hint: lAy = plAce, lIe = reclIne. (A possible source of confusion is that the past tense of lie is lay.)

loose/lose

Loose is the opposite of tight.

> The lid on the jar is loose.

Lose is the present form of lost.

> Stay close so we don't lose you in the crowd.

of/have

Be careful whenever **could of, should of, would of, might of, or must of** appear in your writing. It almost always indicates an incorrect use of **could have, should have, would have, might have, and must have.**

Incorrect: I could of won if that guy hadn't tripped me.

Correct: I could have (could've) won if that guy hadn't tripped me.

Incorrect: I should of gone to Hawaii with my friends.

Correct: I should've (should have) gone to Hawaii with my friends.

passed/past

Passed is the past tense of the verb "to pass."

I passed that car on the freeway yesterday.

Past refers to time

There is something suspicious about her past.

Past also indicates "beyond."

Go past the next light, then turn right.

principal/principle

Principal means "main," like the main administrator of a school.

The principal reason for this problem is bad planning.

The principal will direct the assembly today.

Principle is an ideal or truth.

I won't lie to you because it is against my principles.

Hint: The princiPAL is your pal.

sense/since

Sense relates to:

Perception

I sense your frustration.

Intelligence, reason

Use common sense.

That doesn't make sense.

A "feel" for how something works

sense of humor

sense of justice

Since relates to:

Time

We haven't eaten since noon.

Because

Since we haven't eaten, let's take a lunch break.

than/then

Than indicates comparison: better than, worse than, taller than, colder than, etc.

I like apples more than oranges.

Then indicates sequence or consequence: First_____ then _____. If ___, then_____.

We went to the store then the post office.

If you don't study for the test, then you won't pass this class.

Hint: The word compAre contains the letter A just like thAn. The words sequEnce and consequEnce contain the letter E just like thEn.

their/there/they're

Their shows possession.

I just love their new car.

There indicates place or existence.

Put the cup right there. (indicates place)

There is a problem. (indicates existence)

They're is a contraction of the words they are.

> They're the nicest people you will ever meet.

Hint: The word *their* has an "I" in it, and "I" like to possess things.

to/too

Too means also or indicates an excess of something.

> I like to go to the movies too. (also)

> That movie had too much violence. (excess)

To should be used in all other cases.

weather/whether

Weather relates to atmospheric conditions.

> I hope the weather is nice today.

Whether introduces an option.

> It doesn't matter whether or not you agree with me.

wear/where

Wear relates to clothing or carrying anything upon one's person.

> I usually don't wear earrings.

Where indicates place.

> I want to live where wild animals roam free.

were/we're

Were is a past tense form of the verb to be.

> We were at the party together last night.

We're is a contraction of we are.

We're going to win the lottery any day now.

whose/who's

Whose shows possession.

Whose jacket is this?

Who's is a contraction for who is.

Who's going to the movie with me?

Confused Words—Exercise A

Choose the correct word.

1. I **accepted**/**excepted** John's dinner invitation before he even finished getting the question out.

2. Connie was sure that was against the **principals**/**principles** of enticing flirtation.

3. I really should **of**/**have** played hard to get.

4. Unfortunately, I was **conscience**/**conscious** of my mistake all through the date.

5. When he picked me up, I was so distracted I walked right **passed**/**past** his car.

6. Luckily, as we drove to the restaurant, he eased my nerves by talking **to**/**too** me about the game last week.

7. When we got **their**/**there**/**they're**, I tried to be alluring over dinner, but I think I was trying **to**/**too** hard.

8. He was so polite that I'm not sure **weather**/**whether** or not he even noticed my blunders.

9. That's why I've been waiting for a call from him ever **sense**/**since**.

10. Still, I'm pretty nervous; I hope I didn't **loose**/**lose** my chance with him.

Confused Words—Exercise B

Choose the correct word.

1. **Are/Our** planet has been invaded by a bunch of aliens.

2. The **weather/whether** has taken a turn for the worse.

3. Have you noticed the stuff people **wear/where** lately? It's more **than/then** I can handle.

4. **Their/There/They're** having a crazy **affect/effect** on us!

5. You need to go a little **farther/further** down the road.

6. **Were/We're** in huge trouble.

7. I don't know **wear/where** to find help.

8. I am a little too familiar with my school **principle's/principal's** office.

9. I can't figure out **whose/who's** coming and **whose/who's** not.

10. My **conscience/conscious** is telling me something has **to/too** be done.

Confused Words—Exercise C

Choose the correct word.

1. **Its/It's** my dream to have a brand new puppy, and my family just got one!

2. Six days have **passed/past**, and we've already had our **feel/fill** of puppy-problems.

3. I **accept/except** full responsibility for her misbehavior, **sense/since** I'm the one who is supposed to be training her.

4. That is, **accept/except** for when she chewed up the carpet in the doorway to **are/our** spare bedroom. I don't know **whose/who's** fault that was, but I refuse to believe it was mine.

5. I admit that I'm not always **conscience/conscious** of when she has to "go," so she's left a lot of messes around the house.

6. I want her to **wear/where** her collar, but she keeps gnawing at it.

7. In fact, all my shoe laces are **loose/lose** because she chews them every chance she gets.

8. The worst part is that whenever I try to **lay/lie** down to sleep, she always wants to play, and it's having an **affect/effect** on me.

9. She really is sweeter **than/then** I make her sound, though.

10. I'm just realizing that I really don't know the **principal/principle** behind training yet.

Confused Words—Exercise D

Choose the correct word.

1. **Whose/Who's** awesome? You **are/our**.

2. Just **accept/except** it.

3. **Its/It's** really impressive how far you've come.

4. It's going to have a great **affect/effect** on your grammar.

5. Don't worry, there isn't much **farther/further** to go in the book.

6. You can **feel/fill** confident about that.

7. Look at how much better you are **than/then** you **were/we're** yesterday.

8. It feels good to be **conscience/conscious** of your improvement, right?

9. You're not going to **loose/lose** out on the benefits of grammar.

10. **You're/your** just going to have to keep working.

Answers Key: Confused Words—Exercise A

1. I **accepted** John's dinner invitation before he even finished getting the question out.

2. Connie was sure that was against the **principles** of enticing flirtation.

3. I really should **have** played hard to get.

4. Unfortunately, I was **conscious** of my mistake all through the date.

5. When he picked me up, I was so distracted I walked right **past** his car.

6. Luckily, as we drove to the restaurant, he eased my nerves by talking **to** me about the game last week.

7. When we got **there**, I tried to be alluring over dinner, but I think I was trying **too** hard.

8. He was so polite that I'm not sure **whether** or not he even noticed my blunders.

9. That's why I've been waiting for a call from him ever **since**.

10. Still, I'm pretty nervous; I hope I didn't **lose** my chance with him.

Answers Key: Confused Words—Exercise B

1. **Our** planet has been invaded by a bunch of aliens.

2. The **weather** has taken a turn for the worse.

3. Have you noticed the stuff people **wear** lately? It's more **than** I can handle.

4. **They're** having a crazy **effect** on us!

5. You need to go a little **farther** down the road.

6. **We're** in huge trouble.

7. I don't know **where** to find help.

8. I am a little too familiar with my school **principal's** office.

9. I can't figure out **who's** coming and **who's** not.

10. My **conscience** is telling me something has **to** be done.

Answers Key: Confused Words—Exercise C

1. **It's** my dream to have a brand new puppy, and my family just got one!

2. Six days have **passed**, and we've already had our **fill** of puppy-problems.

3. I **accept** full responsibility for her misbehavior, **since** I'm the one who is supposed to be training her.

4. That is, **except** for when she chewed up the carpet in the doorway to **our** spare bedroom. I don't know **whose** fault that was, but I refuse to believe it was mine.

5. I admit that I'm not always **conscious** of when she has to "go," so she's left a lot of messes around the house.

6. I want her to **wear** her collar, but she keeps gnawing at it.

7. In fact, all my shoe laces are **loose** because she chews them every chance she gets.

8. The worst part is that whenever I try to **lie** down to sleep, she always wants to play, and it's having an **effect** on me.

9. She really is sweeter **than** I make her sound, though.

10. I'm just realizing that I really don't know the **principle** behind training yet.

Answers Key: Confused Words—Exercise D

1. **Who's** awesome? You **are.**

2. Just **accept** it.

3. **It's** really impressive how far you've come.

4. It's going to have a great **effect** on your grammar.

5. Don't worry, there isn't much **further** to go in the book.

6. You can **feel** confident about that.

7. Look at how much better you are **than** you **were** yesterday.

8. It feels good to be **conscious** of your improvement, right?

9. You're not going to **lose** out on the benefits of grammar.

10. **You're** just going to have to keep working.

Commonly Misspelled Words

Good spelling has little correlation to being a good writer; it is possible to be an excellent writer but poor speller. Misspelled words, however, will give your work a sloppy appearance even if the style and composition are brilliant.

English is a hybrid of many different languages and has a colorful past. This results in the various spelling rules and their many exceptions. Learning a few of the most important rules and a few of their exceptions can help you avoid the most common mistakes.

Adding Suffixes

If a word ends in –e and the suffix (letters added to create a new word-ending, like –ing) begins with a vowel, drop the final –e.

    take = taking   phone = phoning   bake = baked   love = lovable

Exception: be = being

If a word ends in a consonant plus –y, change the –y to –i when adding a suffix.

    crazy = crazier   happy = happiest   fry = fried   cry = cried

Exception: The above rule does not apply for –ing.

    fry = frying   cry = crying   supply = supplying

When adding "full" to the end of a word, drop the second –l.

    joyful *not* joyfull   harmful *not* harmfull

"ie" versus "ei"

Perhaps you remember this rule from the rhyme: *Place "i" before "e" except after "c" or when sounded like –ay as in neighbor and weigh.* Here are some examples of when this rule is correct:

i before e: friend, niece, fiend, piece, believe, fierce, die, field

except after c: receive, perceive, deceive, receipt, ceiling

when sounded like –ay: weight, sleigh, feign

Exceptions: being, either, society, weird, leisure, foreign, science, height, seize, protein

Doubling the Final Consonant

If a word is just one syllable and ends in a consonant, double the last letter when adding a suffix.

tag = tagging   flap = flapped   hit = hitter   nap = napping

For two syllable words that end with a single consonant, double the final consonant if the final syllable is stressed.

trans*mit* = transmitted   for*get* = forgetting   im*bed* = imbedded

If the stress falls on the first syllable, the final consonant is not doubled.

*tra*vel = traveled   *mar*vel = marveled

Making Nouns Plural

Most nouns are made plural by simply adding –s to the end.

rock = rocks   bed = beds   flower = flowers   coin = coins

If the noun ends in –s, -z, -x, -sh, -ch, or –ss, then add –es.

boss = bosses   fax = faxes   dish = dishes   match = matches

Exception: quiz = quizzes

For words that end in –f or –fe, change the –f to –v and simply add –es.

life = lives   leaf = leaves   wife = wives

Exceptions: chef = chefs   cliff = cliffs   belief = beliefs   roof = roofs

Using -ible versus -able

How do you know which suffix to use, –ible or –able? The general rule here is that if the root word is Latin-based, then use –ible, and use –able for all other words. Since most of us don't speak Latin, the following guideline may help. Of course, there are exceptions to this guideline, so use a dictionary when in doubt.

If you take away the –ible/–able, is the root word a common English word? If so, then use –able.

Form = formable

Work = workable

Answer = answerable

Value = valuable

Afford = affordable

Comfort = comfortable

If the root word is not a common English word when alone, use –ible. In the following words, the root words alone do not make sense.

compatible	illegible	plausible
comprehensible	incredible	possible
edible	intelligible	responsible
fallible	invisible	sensible
gullible	irresistible	tangible
horrible	permissible	visible

Exceptions: The following words make sense as root words but still take the –ible ending: accessible, defensible, contemptible, digestible, flexible, suggestible

Using Spell Check

Spell check on your word processing program can be a great help, but it is not a perfect solution to spelling errors. Spell check usually does not catch misspellings that form real words, such as from/form. It also does not catch homonyms—words that sound alike but have different meanings and spellings (see Confused Words chapter). A spell checker, for example, may have a hard time dealing with this sentence:

Eye come form a place were wee do knot no how to beet the other team.

American vs. British spelling

Some words have different spellings in American English and British English.

American	British
center	centre
check	cheque
color	colour
gray	grey
labor	labour
neighbor	neighbour
theater	theatre
while	whilst

75 commonly misspelled words

acceptable	fiery	occasionally
accidentally	foreign	occurrence
accommodate	gauge	pastime
acquire	ghost	perseverance
a lot	grateful	personnel
amateur	guarantee	possession
apparent	height	precede
argument	hierarchy	privilege
calendar	humorous	pronunciation
category	immediate	publicly
cemetery	independent	questionnaire
changeable	indispensable	receipt
collectible	intelligence	recommend
column	judgment	referred
committed	colonel	reference
conscience	leisure	restaurant
conscious	liaison	rhyme
consensus	license	rhythm
definitely	maintenance	schedule
discipline	maneuver	sergeant
embarrassment	miniature	supersede
equipment	mischievous	twelfth
exceed	misspell	tyranny
existence	neighbor	until
experience	noticeable	vacuum

Commonly Misspelled Words—Exercise A

Underline and correct any misspelled words.

1. Kick startting the imagination realy is possable.

2. Some beleive that it is amatuer or even harmfull to their inteligance.

3. In reality, it's not so horrable to dicipline the imagination.

4. It requires a lot of maintenence to keep from forgeting how it's done.

5. However, when you get in the habit of useing your imagination, it becomes an irresistable pasttime.

6. People continue imagineing all their lifes.

7. They find themselfs marvelling over simple things like floweres and beliefs.

8. They begin to percieve deeply, even during liesure.

9. They may seem crazyer than most, but they are often happyer too.

10. So, if the urge to imagine siezes you, it is recomended that you act on it.

Commonly Misspelled Words—Exercise B

Underline and correct any misspelled words.

1. I love naping in the afternoones.

2. Occasionily I'm a bit hazyer than normal, and a nap provides imeediate releif.

3. Overall, I think there is a noticable difference.

4. I am less sleeppy.

5. I am more joyfull.

6. I also work more efficeintly.

7. Unfortunately, my skedule doesn't always acomodate a nap.

8. Sometimes I just have to persever.

9. That's why kindergartenerrs are so lucky.

10. For them, takeing a nap is often permissable.

Answer Key: Commonly Misspelled Words—Exercise A

1. Kick <u>starting</u> the imagination <u>really</u> is <u>possible</u>.

2. Some <u>believe</u> that it is <u>amateur</u> or even <u>harmful</u> to their <u>intelligence</u>.

3. In reality, it's not so <u>horrible</u> to <u>discipline</u> the imagination.

4. It requires a lot of <u>maintenance</u> to keep from <u>forgetting</u> how it's done.

5. However, when you get in the habit of <u>using</u> your imagination, it becomes an <u>irresistible</u> <u>pastime</u>.

6. People continue <u>imagining</u> all their <u>lives</u>.

7. They find <u>themselves</u> <u>marveling</u> over simple things like <u>flowers</u> and beliefs.

8. They begin to <u>perceive</u> deeply, even during <u>leisure</u>.

9. They may seem <u>crazier</u> than most, but they are often <u>happier</u> too.

10. So, if the urge to imagine <u>seizes</u> you, it is <u>recommended</u> that you act on it.

Answer Key: Commonly Misspelled Words—Exercise B

1. I love <u>napping</u> in the <u>afternoons</u>.

2. <u>Occasionally</u> I'm a bit <u>hazier</u> than normal, and a nap provides <u>immediate</u> <u>relief</u>.

3. <u>Overall</u>, I think there is a <u>noticeable</u> difference.

4. I am less <u>sleepy</u>.

5. I am more <u>joyful</u>.

6. I also work more <u>efficiently</u>.

7. Unfortunately, my <u>schedule</u> doesn't always <u>accommodate</u> a nap.

8. Sometimes I just have to <u>persevere</u>.

9. That's why <u>kindergarteners</u> are so lucky.

10. For them, <u>taking</u> a nap is often <u>permissible</u>.

Shifts in Time

Every verb has a tense or a time frame in which the action takes place. For example: walk, walked, will walk. Avoid unnecessarily shifting the verb tenses in your writing.

> Incorrect: He **walked** into the house and **opened** the fridge. Suddenly, he **realizes** he **is** not alone.

> Correct: He **walked** into the house and **opened** the fridge. Suddenly, he **realized** he **was** not alone.

Many stories are written in the past tense; however, a writer may choose to relate events in the present tense to create the feeling that events are happening at that moment. This is fine as long it remains consistent.

> Correct: He **walks** into the house and **opens** the fridge. Suddenly, he **realizes** he is not alone.

Acceptable Shifts

Sometimes it is acceptable and necessary to switch tenses. For instance, ongoing facts will be in present tense and completed past actions will be in past tense (even in the same paragraph or sentence).

> Acceptable shift: Drunk driving **is** the leading cause of automobile accidents. **Last year**, more than 16,000 people **died** as a result of drunk driving.

Notice how "is" is present tense because it is discussing an ongoing fact. "Died" is past tense because it is discussing a completed past action last year. The phrase "last year" indicates this transition into past tense.

Novels, Movies, and Articles

When discussing events in a novel or ideas in an essay, use the present tense, even if the author is deceased or the action is set in the distant past.

Hamlet rejects Ophelia because he believes she is deceiving him.

In the essay "Shooting an Elephant," George Orwell describes his experience as an officer in British occupied Burma.

Shifts in Time—Exercise A

Cross out and then correct any unnecessary shifts in tense.

Last week I had a bad first date. I didn't like the movie he wanted to watch, so he suggested another one. It sounded better to me, so we went. He pays for the movie with his laundry money, and we stand in the lobby, waiting for the other movie to get out. He began telling me a personal story and got really loud and animated. As he jumps up and down and waved his arms, I try not to notice the crowd sneaking glances at us. Instead, I prayed I wasn't blushing while nodding and chuckling at the appropriate places. I felt like a giant sign was floating above our heads that said "First Date" in bright, red letters. The movie was worse than I expected. Not only was it boring, he continued to lean closer to me. By the time the movie was over, I am half-way out of my seat, feeling a little sick and ready to be home.

Shifts in Time—Exercise B

Cross out and then correct any unnecessary shifts in tense.

When I was a young child, my family lived next to a cemetery. At first the cemetery never scared me; I just saw it as a fun playground with large stones to climb. When I got older, that changed. The movie that ruined it for me was *Poltergeist*. In the movie, a family lives in a house that was built on top of a cemetery. Ghosts completely took over the house and terrorized the family. In the end, the family moves to get away from the problem. After watching the movie, I can't even look out my bedroom window that faced the cemetery. After that movie, the neighborhood cemetery changed from a fun playground to a forbidden land of restless spirits.

Shifts in Time—Exercise C

Cross out and then correct any unnecessary shifts in tense.

It's interesting to note how people like to live near water. Even people who don't swim or do water sports will pay top dollar for real estate near a lake, river, or ocean. Some speculate that the desire to live near water reflected a primal survival instinct. Long ago, living near water was not just peaceful or beautiful; one's survival depends on it. In our present day, looking out the window and seeing water provides a kind of psychological comfort, even if we didn't have any intention of drinking it or swimming in it.

Answer Key: Shifts in Time—Exercise A

Last week I had a bad first date. I didn't like the movie he wanted to watch, so he suggested another one. It sounded better to me, so we went. He **pays paid** for the movie with his laundry money, and we **stand stood** in the lobby, waiting for the other movie to get out. He began telling me a personal story and got really loud and animated. As he **jumps jumped** up and down and waved his arms, I **try tried** not to notice the crowd sneaking glances at us. Instead, I prayed I wasn't blushing while nodding and chuckling at the appropriate places. I felt like a giant sign was floating above our heads that said "First Date" in bright, red letters. The movie was worse than I expected. Not only was it boring, he continued to lean closer to me throughout it. By the time the movie was over, I **am was** half-way out of my seat, feeling a little sick and ready to be home.

Answer Key: Shifts in Time—Exercise B

When I was a young child, my family lived next to a cemetery. At first the cemetery never scared me; I just saw it as a fun playground with large stones to climb. When I got older, that changed. The movie that ruined it for me was *Poltergeist*. In the movie, a family lives in a house that was built on top of a cemetery. Ghosts completely **took take** over the house and **terrorized terrorize** the family. In the end, the family moves to get away from the problem. After watching the movie, I **can't couldn't** even look out my bedroom window that faced the cemetery. After that movie, the neighborhood cemetery changed from a fun playground to a forbidden land of restless spirits.

Answer Key: Shifts in Time—Exercise C

It's interesting to note how people like to live near water. Even people who don't swim or do water sports will pay top dollar for real estate near a lake, river, or ocean. Some speculate that the desire to live near water **reflected reflects** a primal survival instinct. Long ago, living near water was not just peaceful or beautiful; one's survival **depends depended** on it. In our present day, looking out the window and seeing water provides a kind of psychological comfort, even if we **didn't don't** have any intention of drinking it or swimming in it.

Parallel Structure

To maintain clarity, words or phrases in a list should be in similar (or parallel) form. Don't mix apples with oranges. Imagine a non-parallel sentence looking like this:

> I am going to /, /, and ~.

A parallel sentence would look like this:

> I am going to /, /, and /.

Another factor that creates non-parallel lists is when the base of the sentence (the noun and verb) is awkwardly restated or changed in the list. Consider this non-parallel sentence as a whole, then broken up:

> Not parallel: **I need to** go to the store, drop off the mail, and **the car needs to be** washed.

> **I need to** go to the store.

> **I need to** drop off the mail.

> **I need to** *the car needs to be washed.*

Notice how the base of the sentence "I need to" is changed later in the list: "the car needs to be." An effective way to avoid this change of subject and verb is to imagine listing each item separately before combining the list:

> **I need to** go to the store.

> **I need to** drop off the mail.

> **I need to** wash the car.

> Parallel: I need to go to the store, drop off the mail, and wash the car.

When fixing this mistake, it usually doesn't matter which form you choose, as long as it is consistent.

> Not parallel: In my free time, I like singing and to play the piano.

> Parallel: In my free time, I like singing and playing the piano.

> Also parallel: In my free time, I like to sing and play the piano.

Résumés

Items in separate lists should also be parallel. This problem often occurs in résumés, and reflects poorly on the applicant.

Not parallel:

> Leadership Experience

- **Volunteered** as a reading tutor at Sunnyside Elementary
- **Served** as student body president
- **I have worked** as a mentor at a school for troubled youth

Parallel:

> Leadership Experience

- **Volunteered** as a reading tutor at Sunnyside Elementary
- **Served** as student body president
- **Worked** as a mentor at a school for troubled youth

Parallel Structure—Exercise A

Correct the following sentences for parallelism. Not all sentences require correction.

1. I like the ocean better than going to a lake.
2. I love going to the beach, playing in the sand, and to swim in the ocean.
3. Ice cream tastes the best when it is not too frozen, melted, or tastes too sweet.
4. Lying out in the sun, eating hot dogs, and drinking lemonade are the best

beach activities.

5. Remember to pack the sunscreen, towels, and make sure you have water.

6. I find it the most fun when my family, best friends, and dog all come along.

7. My friend not only knows how to surf, but also scuba diving.

8. To him, to surf is to live life to the fullest.

9. Learning surfing and how to scuba dive are both on my bucket list.

10. Some of the best advantages the beach offers are cute lifeguards and good food.

Parallel Structure—Exercise B

Correct the following lists for parallelism. Not all lists require correction.

1. Instructions for care:

   - Wash cold

   - Use gentle cycle

   - Tumble dry

   - Fabric needs to be ironed

2. Qualifications:

   - Certified in CPR

   - Microsoft Excel

   - Trained in martial arts

3. To grow seedlings:

   - Seeds should be carefully selected

   - Plant in fertile soil

   - Water frequently

- Keep in direct sunlight

4. To do list:

   - Walk the dog

   - Vacuum the carpet

   - Put the cat outside

   - Sweep the kitchen

5. You will need to pack the following:

   - Sleeping bag

   - Bring firewood

   - Tent

   - Food

6. In addition to tuition, your scholarship can cover

   - books,

   - boarding, and

   - transportation.

7. You can improve studying if you follow these tips:

   - Listen intently to the teacher

   - Take thorough notes

   - Study in a quiet place

   - Listening to classical music helps

8. Our business is looking for someone with

   - good work ethic,

   - is punctual, and

- a flexible schedule.

9. The ingredients for this bread are

   - water,

   - flour,

   - yeast, and

   - butter.

10. Desk duties:

    - When the phone rings, answer it

    - Write and send memos

    - Make appointments

Parallel Structure—Exercise C

Correct the following sentences for parallelism. Not all sentences require correction.

1. Some people claim that public schools are failing because the test scores are down and classrooms are unruly and dangerous.

2. Parents should be active participants in their child's school, learning, and the classroom.

3. Higher test scores, lowered dropout rates, and to have a safer learning environment are all things that are affected when parents are actively involved with their children's education.

4. With this involvement, children coming from dysfunctional homes and those who have abuse in their homes are helped significantly.

5. Children who have had help with their education are better off than those who have not.

6. Teachers can't be both the parent and being the teacher.

7. Volunteering in the classroom or to sign up for the PTO are great ways for parents to be involved.

8. Helping with homework, encouraging studies, and a positive attitude are also

things parents can participate in.

9. Teachers benefit from active and persistent parent participation.

10. Schools would be better learning environments if there were complete and willing parent involvement.

Parallel Structure—Exercise D

Correct the following sentences for parallelism. Not all sentences require correction.

1. The first Sunday in February is an exciting time and making great memories.

2. Some of my family can't sleep the night before because they are too nervous and ecstatic for the Super Bowl.

3. Because it is such a big event, we buy a lot of food, buying drinks, and anything else we can think of.

4. The Super Bowl is almost as big as Christmas for us.

5. There is a lot of yelling and sometimes we even scream during the big game.

6. Many people enjoy the commercials as much as to watch the game.

7. In my home, muting the commercials is a regular practice during the Super Bowl so we can talk enthusiastically and eager about what has happened in the game so far.

8. I never see my dad yell so loudly and intensely as I do on this long-awaited day.

9. Mom cooks more on this day than she does any cooking on Thanksgiving.

10. Eating, napping, and a lot of talk follow the excitement of the big game.

Answer Key: Parallel Structure—Exercise A

Answers may vary.

1. I like the ocean better than the lake.

2. I love going to the beach, playing in the sand, and swimming in the ocean.

3. Ice cream tastes the best when it is not too frozen, melted, or sweet.

4. Lying out in the sun, eating hot dogs, and drinking lemonade are the best beach activities. **(no change necessary)**

5. Remember to pack the sunscreen, towels, and water.

6. I find it the most fun when my family, best friends, and dog all come along. **(no change necessary)**

7. My friend not only knows how to surf, but also how to scuba dive.

8. To him, to surf is to live life to the fullest. **(no change necessary)**

9. Learning how to surf and scuba dive are both on my bucket list.

10. Some of the best advantages the beach offers are cute lifeguards and good food. **(no change necessary)**

Answer Key: Parallel Structure—Exercise B

Answers may vary.

1. Instructions for care:
   - Wash cold
   - Use gentle cycle
   - Tumble dry
   - Iron fabric

2. Qualifications:
   - Certified in CPR
   - Proficient with Microsoft Excel
   - Trained in martial arts

3. To grow seedlings:
   - Select seeds carefully
   - Plant in fertile soil
   - Water frequently

- Keep in direct sunlight

4. To do list:

    - Walk the dog

    - Vacuum the carpet

    - Put the cat outside

    - Sweep the kitchen

(no change necessary)

5. You will need to pack the following:

    - Sleeping bag

    - Firewood

    - Tent

    - Food

6. In addition to tuition, your scholarship can cover

    - books,

    - boarding, and

    - transportation.

(no change necessary)

7. You can improve studying if you follow these tips:

    - Listen intently to the teacher

    - Take thorough notes

    - Study in a quiet place

    - Listen to classical music

8. Our business is looking for someone with

    - good work ethic,

    - punctuality, and

- a flexible schedule.

9. The ingredients for this bread are

   - water,

   - flour,

   - yeast, and

   - butter.

(no change necessary)

10. Desk duties:

    - Answer the phone

    - Write and send memos

    - Make appointments

Answer Key: Parallel Structure—Exercise C

Answers may vary.

1. Some people claim that public schools are failing because the test scores are down and classrooms are unruly and dangerous. **(no change necessary)**

2. Parents should be active participants in their child's school, learning, and classroom.

3. Higher test scores, lowered dropout rates, and safer learning environment are all things that are affected when parents are actively involved with their children's education.

4. With this involvement, children coming from dysfunctional and abusive homes are helped significantly.

5. Children who have had help with their education are better off than those who have not. **(no change necessary)**

6. Teachers can't be both the parent and the teacher.

7. Volunteering in the classroom or in the PTO are great ways for parents to be involved.

8. Helping with homework, encouraging studies, and a having a positive attitude are also things parents can participate in.

9. Teachers benefit from active and persistent parent participation. **(no change necessary)**

10. Schools would be better learning environments if there were complete and willing parent involvement. **(no change necessary)**

Answer Key: Parallel Structure—Exercise D

Answers may vary.

1. The first Sunday in February is an exciting time and a chance to make great memories.

2. Some of my family can't sleep the night before because they are too nervous and ecstatic for the Super Bowl. **(no change necessary)**

3. Because it is such a big event, we buy a lot of food, drinks, and anything else we can think of.

4. The Super Bowl is almost as big as Christmas for us. **(no change necessary)**

5. There is a lot of yelling and sometimes even screaming during the big game.

6. Many people enjoy the commercials as much as the actual game.

7. In my home, muting the commercials is a regular practice during the Super Bowl so we can talk enthusiastically and eagerly about what has happened in the game so far.

8. I never see my dad yell so loudly and intensely as I do on this long-awaited day. **(no change necessary)**

9. Mom cooks more on this day than she does on Thanksgiving.

10. Eating, napping, and talking follow the excitement of the big game.

Problems with Pronouns

A pronoun replaces a noun with words like she, they, your, their, it, etc. We use these words to avoid repetition.

> No pronoun: **Students** can view the **students'** grades online.

> Pronoun: **Students** can view **their** grades online. (*Their* replaces *students*.)

> No pronoun: **My computer** was broken, so I asked my roommate to fix **my computer.**

> Pronoun: **My computer** was broken, so I asked my roommate to fix **it.** (*It* replaces *my computer*.)

Shift in Person

"Person" refers to the "who" of a sentence. Review the following first, second, and third person pronouns to get a feel for these categories.

> **1st person singular:** I, my, me

> **1st person plural:** we, our, us

> **2nd person singular:** you, your

> **2nd person plural:** you (Informally expressed "you guys"), your

> **3rd person singular:** he, she, his, her, him, it, its

> **3rd person plural:** they, their, them

Avoid unnecessarily changing the "person" in sentences or paragraphs.

> Unnecessary Shift: Many **parents** spank **their** children out of anger and frustration, but this is no excuse. **You** must first calm down before deciding how to discipline **your** children. (Notice the shift from 3rd person plural [parents, their] to 2nd person [you, your])

Better: Many **parents** spank **their** children out of anger and frustration, but this is no excuse. **They** must first calm down before deciding how to discipline **their** children.

Unnecessary Shift: If **a student** wants an exciting summer job, **they** can work in a national park. **You** won't earn a lot of money, but the recreational opportunities are amazing. (Notice the shift from 3rd person singular [a student] to 3rd person plural [they], then to 2nd person [you].)

Better: If **students** want to earn extra money during the summer, **they** can work in a national park. **They** won't earn a lot of money, but the recreation opportunities are amazing.

Many shifts in person are logical and necessary. In the following example, the first person singular (I) remembers good times with a first person plural (we).

Correct: My friends are gone now, but I will never forget the good times we had our last summer together.

The General "You"

To avoid sounding pompous, some writers use "you" instead of "one" to refer to a non-specific person. Depending on the formality of the writing, this can be acceptable when used sparingly and when the sentence is an obvious generalization.

Acceptable: When someone yells "fire" in a crowded building, **you** don't stick around to ask questions.

However, repeatedly addressing the reader as "you" can sound accusatory, as if pointing your finger directly at the reader.

Accusatory: Once **you** understand the causes of obesity, **you** can start changing your lifestyle.

Better: Once **people** understand the causes of obesity, **they** can start changing their lifestyle.

The following sentences use different ways of generalizing the person. One version is not necessarily correct or incorrect, but each has a slightly different effect. The audience and the formality of the writing also play a role in which version to choose.

When it comes to recycling, **one** can always do better.

When it comes to recycling, **we** can always do better.

When it comes to recycling, **people** can always do better.

Pronoun Agreement in Number

A common error is to use "they" (a plural pronoun) when referring to a singular noun. While this may be considered normal in everyday speech, avoid it in formal writing.

Incorrect: I hate it when **a customer** doesn't know what **they** want.

Correct: I hate it when **customers** don't know what **they** want.

Also: I hate it when **a customer** doesn't know what **he or she** wants.

Sexist Use of Pronouns

Avoid favoring one gender when referring to nonspecific persons. This mistake is especially common in stereotyping particular professions or activities as essentially male or female.

A good doctor will always listen to **his** patients. (What about the female doctors?)

A student must apply to the **nursing program** if **she** wishes to become a nurse. (Men are also nurses.)

An effective solution, when possible, is to make the noun and pronouns plural so they become gender neutral.

Better: Good **doctors** will always listen to **their** patients.

Better: **Students** must apply to the nursing program if **they** wish to become nurses.

Another possibility is to rephrase the sentence completely.

Listening to patients is the hallmark of a good doctor.

Students who want to become nurses must apply to the nursing program.

The following examples represent additional options. However, these constructions can be awkward and wordy. Avoid using these constructions unless completely necessary.

A good doctor will always listen to **his/her** patients.

A student must apply to the nursing program if **he or she** wishes to become a nurse.

Who vs. That

Use the pronoun "who" when referring to people, "that" when referring to things, "when" when referring to time, and "where" when referring to places.

Incorrect: I know a man **that** climbed Mount Everest.

Correct: I know a man **who** climbed Mount Everest.

Incorrect: Is there a time **that** you can come to my house?

Correct: Is there a time **when** you can come to my house?

Vague Pronouns

Remember that a pronoun replaces a noun, so that instead of saying, "My roommate dropped off his car so that I could fix the car," we say, "My roommate dropped off his car so that I could fix it." "It" replaces "car." Problems arise when it is not clear which noun the pronoun replaces.

Vague: My roommate dropped off his car and computer so that I could fix **it**. (What does "it" refer to, the car or the computer?)

Better: My roommate dropped off his computer for me to repair. He also dropped off his car.

This

The word "this" can cause confusion because it can refer to anything—a phenomenon, situation, or group of things.

Vague: The music at the concert was too loud and the crowd was too wild. The food was terrible, and it rained for two hours. **This** made me feel sick the next day. (Does "this" refer to any single thing or the whole set of circumstances?)

Better: The music at the concert was too loud and the crowd was too wild. The food was terrible, and it rained for two hours. The bad food and chilly weather made me feel sick the next day.

That

Make sure it is clear whether "that" refers to many things or one thing specifically.

Vague: He said he got stuck in traffic and blew a tire. He also said he ran out of gas just before he arrived. **That** seems pretty unlikely to me.

Better: He said he got stuck in traffic and blew a tire. He also said he ran out of gas just before he arrived. Running out of gas seems pretty unlikely to me.

Also: He said he got stuck in traffic and blew a tire. He also said he ran out of gas just before he arrived. It seems unlikely that all these things would happen in one trip.

People

When discussing multiple persons, make sure it is clear who the pronouns "he/she/they/him/her" refer to.

Vague: **My mom and sister** went shopping last night. My mom bought my sister new shoes, but when they came home **she** decided she didn't like them.

Better: **My mom and sister** went shopping last night. My mom bought my sister new shoes, but when they came home **my sister** decided she didn't like them.

Problems with Pronouns—Exercise A

In the following sentences, identify if there is a shift in person and decide if the shift is unnecessary or necessary. If the shift is unnecessary, correct the sentence.

1. Finding a good book is easy if you know where to look. We can always ask a librarian for a recommendation.

2. When I go boating, you should always wear a life vest.

3. My favorite time of year is autumn. It's a good time for you to go on hikes with your friends.

4. We are entitled to our opinion, but you should be considerate when presenting your argument.

5. My siblings and I play a lot of board games. We always compete to see who can win the most games in a row.

Problems with Pronouns—Exercise B

Identify the sentences that use the pronoun "you" in an accusatory way. If it sounds accusatory, correct the sentence by changing the pronoun to "we" or "people," whichever fits. Don't forget to change the verb conjugation if necessary.

1. When it comes to dating, you never know when you'll bump into the "one."

2. It is commonly accepted that whenever you let your dog out in public without a leash, you are risking the safety of your dog and others.

3. If you stopped relying on the government for your food and housing, national debt could be greatly decreased.

4. It just goes to show that you can't judge a book by its cover.

5. Many health benefits come from exercising daily. If you had proper motivation, you would create a daily exercise routine.

Problems with Pronouns—Exercise C

In the following sentences, make the pronouns and subjects agree in number. Some sentences have more than one subject. Don't forget to change the verb conjugation if necessary.

1. A student can always go to the library for all of their research needs.

2. Sometimes the best résumé is the one that appeals to an employer's visual tastes.

3. In order for a patient to be in top shape for giving blood, they must stay hydrated days in advance.

4. When writing a research paper, it is not necessary to ask permission from the author before quoting their work.

5. A homeowner can do many of their own home repairs, but sometimes they need to ask a professional for their opinion.

Problems with Pronouns—Exercise D

In the following sentences, correct gender bias either by making the subject and pronoun plural or by rewording the sentence.

1. A firefighter must always keep track of his gear.

2. By the time a child turns seven, he should know how to tie his shoes.

3. If a student wants to avoid missing his appointments, he should keep a planner with him.

4. A forgetful person may lose her keys often.

5. When people are hospitalized, a nurse and her assistant often tend to them.

Problems with Pronouns—Exercise E

Correct the following sentences so "who" refers to people, "that" refers to things, "when" refers to a time, and "where" refers to a place.

1. She's the one _____ broke my window.

2. It's frustrating to own a car _____ doesn't even work.

3. Do you remember the one time _____ you broke your leg?

4. This is the neighborhood _____ I grew up.

5. Remember the people _____ have died for our country.

Problems with Pronouns—Exercise F

Rewrite the following sentences so that the vague pronouns refer to something specific.

1. The wedding cake arrived late and was covered in teal icing roses. This was very upsetting for the bride.

2. He only wore blue jeans and an old tee shirt on the date, and he brought me flowers and opened the car door for me. That made my day.

3. My professor, Mr. Brown, lives next to my brother. His house is white with

blue shutters.

4. The Small Town Sparrows and The Big City Jackrabbits came head to head in the game of a century. In an incredible turn of events, they won by a land-slide.

5. For Thanksgiving, my sister and my niece came to visit. I made the turkey, stuffing, mashed potatoes and rolls. Unfortunately, she didn't like them.

Answer Key: Problems with Pronouns—Exercise A

1. Finding a good book is easy if you know where to look. **You** can always ask a librarian for a recommendation.

2. When I go boating, **I** should always wear a life vest.

3. My favorite time of year is autumn. It's a good time for **me** to go on hikes with **my** friends.

4. We are entitled to our opinion, but **we** should be considerate when presenting **our** argument.

5. My siblings and I play a lot of board games. We always compete to see who can win the most games in a row. **(no change necessary)**

Answer Key: Problems with Pronouns—Exercise B

1. When it comes to dating, you never know when you'll bump into the "one." **(no change necessary)**

2. It is commonly accepted that whenever **people let their** dog out in public without a leash, **they** are risking the safety of **their** dog and others.

OR

It is commonly accepted that whenever **we let our dogs** out in public without a leash, **we** are risking the safety of **our dogs** and others.

3. If **people** stopped relying on the government for **their** food and housing, na-tional debt could be greatly decreased.

OR

If **we** stopped relying on the government for **our** food and housing, national debt could be greatly decreased.

4. It just goes to show that you can't judge a book by its cover. **(no change necessary)**

5. Many health benefits come from exercising daily. If **people** had proper motivation, **they** would create a daily exercise routine.

    OR

    Many health benefits come from exercising daily. If **we** had proper motivation, **we** would create a daily exercise routine.

Answer Key: Problems with Pronouns—Exercise C

1. **Students** can always go to the library for all of their research needs.

2. Sometimes the best résumé is the one that appeals to employer's visual tastes.

3. In order for **patients** to be in top shape for giving blood, they must stay hydrated days in advance.

4. When writing a research paper, it is not necessary to ask permission from **authors** before quoting their work.

5. **Homeowners** can do many of their own home repairs, but sometimes they need to ask **professionals** for their opinion.

Answer Key: Problems with Pronouns—Exercise D

Answers may vary.

1. **Firefighters** must always keep track of **their** gear.

2. By the time **children turn** seven, **they** should know how to tie **their** shoes.

3. If **students want** to avoid missing **their** appointments, **they** should keep a planner with **them**.

4. Forgetful **people** may lose **their** keys often.

5. When people are hospitalized, **nurses** and **their assistants** often tend to them.

Answer Key: Problems with Pronouns—Exercise E

1. She's the one **who** broke my window.

2. It's frustrating to own a car **that** doesn't even work.

3. Do you remember the one time **when** you broke your leg?

4. This is the neighborhood **where** I grew up.

5. Remember the people **who** have died for our country.

Answer Key: Problems with Pronouns—Exercise F

Answers may vary.

1. The wedding cake arrived late and was covered in teal icing roses. Because it was late, the bride was upset.

2. He only wore blue jeans and an old tee shirt on the date, and he brought me flowers and opened the car door for me. The flowers made my day.

3. My professor, Mr. Brown, lives next to my brother. Mr. Brown's house is white with blue shutters.

4. The Small Town Sparrows and The Big City Jackrabbits came head to head in the game of a century. In an incredible turn of events, The Sparrows won by a landslide.

5. For Thanksgiving, my sister and my niece came to visit. I made the turkey, stuffing, mashed potatoes and rolls. Unfortunately, my niece didn't like the mashed potatoes.

Capitalization

First Words

Capitalize the first word of every sentence. This rule applies to emails and online communications as well.

> Do not feed the alligator.

> Professor Smith, I have a question.

Direct Quotations or Dialogue

Capitalize the first word of a quotation, even if it occurs in the middle of another sentence.

> As Mark Twain once said, "Nothing so needs reforming as other people's habits."

Do not capitalize the first word if the quotation is the completion of a previously started sentence.

> "Nothing so needs reforming," Mark Twain once said, "as other people's habits."

Major Words in Titles

Capitalize the first words of titles and all nouns and verbs. Do not capitalize "the" or prepositions if they occur mid-title.

> *Where the Red Fern Grows*

> "Ode on a Grecian Urn"

Countries, Languages, Nationalities

Spain

French

English history and American literature

Racial and Ethnic Groups

Do not capitalize the general categories of "black" and "white." (Not all guides agree on this point.)

Asian

Native-American

white

Europeans

black

Americans

Names and Titles

Capitalize titles when used in place of a person's name or when attached to a person's name.

Have you talked to Mom yet? Let's invite Aunt Jane for dinner.

In history today, Professor Smith was late.

Do not capitalize titles when not acting as a name or when not associated with a specific person's name.

To test if a title is acting as a name, replace it with your name. For example, "I talked to Mom" would make sense as "I talked to Josh" would. But "I talked to my mom" could not be "I talked to my Josh." Since it sounds awkward with a name replacing the title, you know it is not acting as a name and should not be capitalized.

I invited my aunt to dinner.

The history professor was late for class.

Academic Subjects

Capitalize academic subjects only when their names are based on countries or languages, or when they indicate a specific class, not just a general subject.

Have you taken Psychology 201?

I like my American literature class.

I am not a fan of history.

I wish I had a better time slot for Science 101.

Proper Nouns

Capitalize the names of specific companies, brands, and institutions.

General Electric   Boeing   Republican Party   American Civil Liberties Union

Religion

Capitalize specific religions or names of deity. General references like "the gods" are not capitalized. (Some styles also capitalize pronouns that refer to deity.)

I am Catholic, and he is Mormon.

Are you Christian?

Buddha taught powerful truths.

I believe in Jesus Christ and His teachings.

Dates

Capitalize days of the week, months, and holidays. Do not capitalize seasons. (*Capitalize what is found on a calendar.*)

Monday

March

Christmas

winter, spring, summer, and fall

Locations

Capitalize the names of specific locations, cities, and street names. Do not capitalize general directions.

Madison Hospital

Elm Street

Rocky Mountains

I live in the South. (as a location)

I turned west. (as a direction)

Capitalization—Exercise A

Capitalize every word that needs to be capitalized.

1. I want to read to kill a mockingbird.

2. I wish I could go live in the south because I love eggs and grits.

3. How on earth does one get to federal avenue?

4. What is your mom's name?

5. Was that your uncle bill in that truck?

6. Do you speak russian?

7. I want to skip my chemistry class so that I can finish my homework for english.

8. My hardest class is math 101.

9. I told mom that I want to live at home forever.

10. Have you ever been to a muslim mosque?

Capitalization—Exercise B

Capitalize every word that needs to be capitalized.

1. have you ever been to the black forests of russia? i don't mean a specific forest, for this is a type of forest known all through the country.

2. in russia, a black forest refers to any wooded area made of deciduous trees. you see, the trees appear black in the winter when all the leaves have fallen and just the wet bark is seen against the snow.

3. i've always imagined that baba yaga would have lived in such a forest.

4. she is a character in one of the oldest pieces of slavic folklore.

5. i think i first heard of baba yaga when i was around ten years old, just as the school year finished in may.

6. my mother brought home a thin book with marvelous illustrations, most of them filled with a strange, skeletal woman grinning with flat lips.

7. the lady's skin was somewhat olive-colored.

8. it was not until later that i learned that her skin was supposed to be graying with decomposition.

9. in old russian, the word *baba* can refer to a midwife, sorceress, or even a fortune teller.

10. even in modern russian, her name is in the common language: *babushka* is the word used to refer to grandmothers.

Capitalization—Exercise C

Capitalize every word that needs to be capitalized.

1. My birthday is in the fall, specifically october 23, which falls on a tuesday this year.

2. In my class on world religions we are learning about buddhism.

3. My brother likes to go to mcdonald's on his birthday.

4. It's our family tradition to go out for asian food the day before thanksgiving.

5. I want to go mountain biking in a national park for spring break this year.

6. The novel don quixote is set in spain.

7. American airlines offers flights to most european countries.

8. Easter island is one of the most remote places on the planet.

9. I watched a documentary about the ancient romans on the history channel.

10. We listened to a speech by spiderman, the current president of the insect rights society.

Answer Key: Capitalization—Exercise A

1. I want to read *To Kill a Mockingbird*.

2. I wish I could go live in the South because I love eggs and grits.

3. How on earth does one get to Federal Avenue?

4. What is your mom's name? (no change)

5. Was that your Uncle Bill in that truck?

6. Do you speak Russian?

7. I want to skip my chemistry class so that I can finish my homework for English.

8. My hardest class is Math 101.

9. I told Mom that I want to live at home forever.

10. Have you ever been to a Muslim mosque?

Answer Key: Capitalization—Exercise B

1. Have you ever been to the black forests of Russia? I don't mean a specific forest, for this is a type of forest known all through the country.

2. In Russia, a black forest refers to any wooded area made of deciduous trees. You see, the trees appear black in the winter when all the leaves have fallen and just the wet bark is seen against the snow.

3. I've always imagined that Baba Yaga would have lived in such a forest.

4. She is a character in one of the oldest pieces of Slavic folklore.

5. I think I first heard of Baba Yaga when I was around ten years old, just as the school year finished in May.

6. My mother brought home a thin book with marvelous illustrations, most of them filled with a strange, skeletal woman grinning with flat lips.

7. The lady's skin was somewhat olive-colored.

8. It was not until later that I learned that her skin was supposed to be graying with decomposition.

9. In old Russian, the word *baba* can refer to a midwife, sorceress, or even a fortune teller.

10. Even in modern Russian, her name is in the common language: *babushka* is the word used to refer to grandmothers.

Answer Key: Capitalization—Exercise C

1. My birthday is in the fall, specifically October 23, which falls on a Tuesday this year.

2. In my class on world religions we are learning about Buddhism.

3. My brother likes to go to McDonald's on his birthday.

4. It's our family tradition to go out for Asian food the day before Thanksgiving.

5. I want to go mountain biking in a national park for spring break this year. (no change)

6. The novel *Don Quixote* is set in Spain.

7. American Airlines offers flights to most European countries.

8. Easter Island is one of the most remote places on the planet.

9. I watched a documentary about the ancient Romans on the History Channel.

10. We listened to a speech by Spiderman, the current president of the Insect Rights Society.

Apostrophes

Apostrophes are punctuation marks (') that generally work to make a word possessive or to indicate a contraction.

To indicate possession

Bob's company   Sally's bagels   the children's playground

Tess's Beauty Salon   the student's book   Ross's new car

To show possession for a plural word that ends in *-s* just add an apostrophe after the -s.

the students' books (multiple students)   the movie stars' autographs (multiple stars)

Note: The apostrophe only comes at the end of the word when the word shows plural possession by ending in -s (e.g. students'). When the word is singular and possessive, it is followed by an extra -s. (*Ross's new car* not *Ross' new car*.) Some guides disagree on the details of showing possesion using apostrophes. If writing for publication, follow the house style guide.

To indicate a contraction

can't   doesn't   they're

wouldn't   we're   it's (it is)

To avoid confusion

Sometimes a writer will refer to a word *as a word* in a text. To avoid suggesting that such words are in plural form, an apostrophe can be used.

When proofreading the essay, I found too many *that*'s and *however*'s.

When not to use an apostrophe

Do not use an apostrophe to create a plural. Instead, add *s* or *–es*.

the 1960s my pencils   ten DVDs

the masses kites   dishes

Do not add an apostrophe to verbs. Errors commonly occur with "sees" and "says."

Incorrect: She see's her faults.

Correct: She sees her faults.

Incorrect: He say's he's a nice guy.

Correct: He says he's a nice guy.

Do not add an apostrophe to possessive pronouns. These words already indicate possession, so an apostrophe is not necessary.

yours   hers   its   theirs   ours

Note: A very common error is to confuse *its* and *it's*. It is tempting to think the one with the apostrophe indicates possession because, after all, that's what apostrophes do. But remember that *its* is already a possessive pronoun, and *it's* is a contraction of "it is."

Apostrophes–Exercise A

Underline all the incorrect punctuation and correct it.

1. Youre not the only one in the room.

2. My boss' new office has inflated his ego.

3. I love books from the 1800's.

4. So, whatll you have for dinner?

5. You don't have your friends phone number anymore.

6. The mass's are all going shopping after Thanksgiving.

7. Its hard to believe that buckling your seatbelt would help much during a plane crash.

8. Is that new car your's or your dads?

9. Youll find out soon enough its not worth it.

10. The neighbors said the barking dog isnt their's.

Apostrophes–Exercise B

Underline all the incorrect punctuation and correct it. Some sentences are already correct.

1. Karate is a good sport for kid's.

2. Have you considered all of it's benefit's?

3. It's good for kids self-discipline.

4. They learn a life skill and become healthier.

5. It also build's confidence.

6. Of course, activitie's shouldn't take priority over the familys time.

7. But if its all kept in balance, kid's generally enjoy karate.

8. They dont learn to fight so much as gain self-control.

9. Your childrens attitude will even improve.

10. It beat's sitting in front of the TV.

Apostrophes–Exercise C

Underline all the incorrect punctuation and correct it. Some sentences are already correct.

1. Recently, I had some out-of-town guest's.

2. I cleaned all the room's in my house until they were spotless.

3. Its amazing how many things hadnt been cleaned in ages.

4. I guess it takes other's to motivate me.

5. I did the dish's, floor's, and window's.

6. Soon, my house looked like my mother's in the 1960's, spotless.

7. As my mother always say's, "Hard work pay's off."

8. She's right, of course.

9. When my guests arrived and complimented my home, I didnt have any *buts* to add. It really did look great.

10. Id worked hard, and itd paid off.

Answer Key: Apostrophes—Exercise A

1. <u>You're</u> not the only one in the room.

2. My <u>boss's</u> new office has inflated his ego.

3. I love books from the <u>1800s</u>.

4. So, <u>what'll</u> you have for dinner?

5. You don't have your <u>friend's</u> phone number anymore.

6. The <u>masses</u> are all going shopping after Thanksgiving.

7. <u>It's</u> hard to believe that buckling your seatbelt would help much during a plane crash.

8. Is that new car <u>yours</u> or your <u>dad's</u>?

9. <u>You'll</u> find out soon enough <u>it's</u> not worth it.

10. The neighbors said the barking dog <u>isn't</u> <u>theirs</u>.

Answer Key: Apostrophes—Exercise B

1. Karate is a good sport for <u>kids</u>.

2. Have you considered all of <u>its</u> benefits?

3. It's good for <u>kids'</u> self-discipline.

4. They learn a life skill and become healthier. (no change)

5. It also <u>builds</u> confidence.

6. Of course, <u>activities</u> shouldn't take priority over the <u>family's</u> time.

7. But if <u>it's</u> all kept in balance, <u>kids</u> generally enjoy karate.

8. They <u>don't</u> learn to fight so much as gain self-control.

9. Your <u>children's</u> attitude will even improve.

10. It <u>beats</u> sitting in front of the TV.

Answer Key: Apostrophes–Exercise C

1. Recently, I had some out-of-town <u>guests</u>.

2. I cleaned all the <u>rooms</u> in my house until they were spotless.

3. <u>It's</u> amazing how many things <u>hadn't</u> been cleaned in ages.

4. I guess it takes <u>others</u> to motivate me.

5. I did the <u>dishes</u>, <u>floors</u>, and <u>windows</u>.

6. Soon, my house looked like my mother's in the <u>1960s</u>, spotless.

7. As my mother always <u>says</u>, "Hard work <u>pays</u> off."

8. She's right, of course. **(no change necessary)**

9. When my guests arrived and complimented my home, I <u>didn't</u> have any <u>but's</u> to add. It really did look great.

10. <u>I'd</u> worked hard, and <u>it'd</u> paid off.

Subject-Verb Agreement

Remember that a complete sentence requires a verb and a subject—or "action" and a subject doing the action. In most cases, the verb changes form depending on the nature of the subject. Subject – verb agreement just means that the subject and verb correctly match in their corresponding form.

> I go jogging every day. NOT I goes jogging every day.

> They run the river once per summer. NOT They runs the river once per summer.

Interfering Prepositions

In the above examples, it's easy to see the error and identify the correct sentence. Sometimes, however, it's harder to identify the subject of the sentence and determine whether the subject is singular or plural. Even though some of the words below seem to indicate a plurality of people or things, they are singular when used as subjects.

Anyone	Each	Everything
Everyone	Nobody	Somebody
No one	Everybody	Anybody
Someone		

When a prepositional phrase (a phrase depending on a preposition, such as *in*) comes between one of these subjects and a verb, things get a little trickier. When the object of the preposition is plural, it's tempting to make the verb plural to match. Instead, mentally cross out the prepositional phrase, or anything else that comes between the subject and the verb, to ensure agreement.

> Tempting: Everything about the new **curtains have** to be changed.

> Correct: **Everything** ~~about the new curtains~~ **has** to be changed.

Tempting: Each of the **cupcakes need** pink frosting.

Correct: **Each** ~~of the cupcakes~~ **needs** pink frosting.

Tempting: Everybody on the freeway in their overheated cars **were** honking.

Correct: **Everybody** ~~on the freeway in their overheated cars~~ **was** honking.

Five words (subject pronouns) make an exception to the above rule: *none, most, all, any,* and *some.* When a preposition comes between one of these subjects and a verb, the word at the end of the prepositional phrase (object of the preposition) determines whether the verb will be plural.

Correct: All of the **leaves have** been raked.

Also correct: All of the **leaf has** been eaten by the insect.

Correct: **Are** any of the **teammates** going to the party?

Also correct: **Is** any of the **syrup** left in the bottle?

Compound Subjects

When a sentence has multiple subjects joined by the word *and*, the subject is plural.

Fresh fruit and water are a good way to start the day.

A warm bath and a cup of hot cocoa make the perfect end to a day of skiing.

When the word *or* joins two subjects, the subject closest to the verb determines whether the verb will be plural or singular.

Either my shoes or **my necklace was** stolen.

Either my necklace or **my shoes were** stolen.

Collective Nouns

Some nouns seem like they indicate multiple people or things, but most often function as a single unit. A few common collective nouns are family, team, nation, gang, herd, committee, and class.

Incorrect: I have a big **family**, and **they are** getting bigger.

Correct: I have a big **family**, and **it is** getting bigger.

Incorrect: The whole football **team are** in need of new helmets.

Correct: The whole football **team is** in need of new helmets.

Also correct: **Each player** on the football team **needs** a new helmet.

Verbs before Subjects

Subjects usually come before the verb in the sentence. Sometimes, however, verbs come before subjects. This most often occurs when a sentence begins with *there's* or *here's*.

Incorrect: **Here's** the **papers** I borrowed.

Correct: **Here are** the **papers** I borrowed. (subject = papers)

Incorrect: **There's** more **sodas** in the fridge.

Correct: **There are** more **sodas** in the fridge. (subject = sodas)

Subject-Verb Agreement–Exercise A

In the following sentences, mentally cross out the words that come between the subject and verb, then indicate whether the subject and verb are in agreement. Not all sentences are incorrect.

(Remember that this is only an exercise to determine subject-verb agreement; there is nothing wrong with additional words coming between subjects and verbs.)

1. Anybody on four wheels are required to be trained.

2. Everything under this roof is in order.

3. Someone from the recruiters call every day.

4. Each of the children are happy.

5. Anything beyond the loading stations are inaccessible.

6. No one but athletes understand this problem.

7. Everybody except weirdoes like pizza.

8. Nobody at these parties ever say hi.

9. Anyone from the States recognize the flag.

10. Everyone in these groups belongs.

Subject-Verb Agreement–Exercise B

The following sentences use compound subjects. Identify and correct sentences that do not have subject-verb agreement. Not all sentences are incorrect.

1. Connie and Julie are coming over.

2. Connie or Julie are coming over.

3. This chair and that rug looks really nice together.

4. Blood, sweat, and tears goes into this.

5. A drill or screwdriver works.

6. Those flip flops or my bathing suit fit in my bag.

7. A hamburger or fries sounds nice right now.

8. Thanksgiving and Christmas approaches!

9. Red bricks or stone are all we have for sale.

10. My keys and wallet are all I need.

Subject-Verb Agreement–Exercise C

The following sentences either use collective nouns or the verb comes before the subject. Identify and correct those sentences that do not have subject-verb agreement. Not all sentences are incorrect.

1. Where's the dogs?

2. The team called; they are meeting down the street.

3. That's true.

4. Check out that herd; it's running wild!

5. The committee want this done immediately.

6. What time are we meeting?

7. The class of 2014 are all grown up.

8. That sound are from wolves howling.

9. The nation is developing.

10. There's mice in this house.

Answer Key: Subject-Verb Agreement–Exercise A

1. **Anybody** on four wheels **is** required to be trained.

2. **Everything** under this roof **is** in order. **(no change necessary)**

3. **Someone** from the recruiters **calls** every day.

4. **Each** of the children **is** happy.

5. **Anything** beyond the loading stations **is** inaccessible.

6. **No one** but athletes **understands** this problem.

7. **Everybody** except weirdoes **likes** pizza.

8. **Nobody** at these parties ever **says** hi.

9. **Anyone** from the States **recognizes** the flag.

10. **Everyone** in these groups **belongs**. **(no change necessary)**

Answer Key: Subject-Verb Agreement–Exercise B

1. **Connie and Julie are** coming over. **(no change necessary)**

2. Connie or **Julie is** coming over.

3. **This chair and that rug look** really nice together.

4. **Blood, sweat, and tears go** into this.

5. A drill or **screwdriver works**. **(no change necessary)**

6. Those flip flops or my **bathing suit fits** in my bag.

7. A hamburger or **fries sound** nice right now.

8. **Thanksgiving and Christmas approach**!

9. Red bricks or **stone is** all we have for sale.

10. **My keys and wallet are** all I need. **(no change necessary)**

Answer Key: Subject-Verb Agreement–Exercise C

1. Where **are** the **dogs**?

2. The **team** called; **it's** meeting down the street.

3. **That's true. (no change necessary)**

4. Check out that **herd**; **it's** running wild! **(no change necessary)**

5. The **committee wants** this done immediately.

6. What time **are we** meeting? **(no change necessary)**

7. The class of 2014 **is** all grown up.

8. That sound **is** from wolves howling.

9. The **nation is** developing. **(no change necessary)**

10. **There are mice** in this house.

Other Punctuation

Miscellaneous Punctuation

This section covers items that do not warrant a chapter of their own but that are still important to know. It's the equivalent of that drawer in your house that collects everything that doesn't belong neatly in other drawers.

Semicolon

Use a semicolon instead of a period to show a close relationship between two sentences; the second sentence serves as a kind of follow-up thought. Make sure the first AND second sentences can stand alone as complete sentences (independent clauses). Remember, if you can't put a period there, you can't put a semicolon there either.

> I love studying grammar; it's the best.

Semicolons can also be used for complex lists to avoid confusing items intended as pairs.

> Confusing: Last summer I travelled to New York, Paris, France, Rome, Italy and Moscow, Russia.

> Better: Last summer I travelled to New York; Paris, France; Rome, Italy; and Moscow, Russia.

Colon

Use a colon to indicate that a list or specific information will follow. A colon does not integrate this information smoothly into a sentence. A colon creates an abrupt stop. It's as if it says, "The information I am about to give you will follow this mark : "

> Our new dog finally has a name: Edwin.

> The following vegetables contain calcium: spinach, kale, broccoli, and okra.

Do not use a colon if the list or information is integrated into the sentence.

> We finally gave our new dog the name of Edwin.

> Some vegetables that contain calcium are spinach, kale, broccoli, and okra.

Parentheses

Use parentheses to interject additional information that is a slight interruption to your line of thought. You should be able to remove whatever is in the parentheses and the sentence should still make sense. Keep in mind that parentheses are fairly intrusive, so they should be avoided for academic or professional writing.

> When I went to New York last summer (first time ever), I didn't get to see the Statue of Liberty.

> Twenty years ago (could it be that long?) when I entered college, we didn't have the internet.

Dash

A dash can be used to indicate inserted additional information, almost as a "softer" parentheses.

> On our way back we saw another deer—we had seen several—standing in the middle of the road.

A dash can also create a dramatic pause to emphasize additional information at the end of a sentence.

> When we returned from vacation, our cat presented us with a little surprise—a litter of kittens.

Exclamation point

Use exclamation points to indicate strong emotion, mostly in informal writing. This mark gives a sense of urgency or even loudness to a sentence.

Exclamation points are often abused and overused in settings such as email and social media. Resist the temptation to use multiple exclamation points after one sentence or to put exclamation points after nearly every sentence.

> Adequate: I heard you got accepted into law school. That is wonderful!

> Overdone: I heard you got accepted into law school!!! That is wonderful!!!!

Question mark

Use a question mark after—you guessed it—a question. A common mistake is to put a question mark after indirect questions.

Statement: I wonder what we are eating tonight.

Question: What are we going to eat tonight?

Statement: Dad asked me where you took the car last night.

Question: Where did you take the car last night?

Junk Drawer–Exercise A

Identify and correct any misuse of semi-colons below. Not all sentences are incorrect.

1. I hope they arrive today; that would be wonderful.

2. That picture is phenomenal; and it's the original.

3. I'd really like to visit Tokyo, Japan, Christchurch, New Zealand, and Johannesburg, South Africa.

4. Whenever I take a nap; I always feel great.

5. The meeting times are at 4:30, today, 5:30, tomorrow, and 6:30, Wednesday.

Junk Drawer–Exercise B

Identify and correct any misuse of colons below. Not all sentences are incorrect.

1. The ingredients I will use are: carrots, parsnips, and nutmeg.

2. This is my favorite thing: sleeping in.

3. Don't forget the following items, sunscreen, bug spray, and matches.

4. It's time: to say sorry.

5. On our picnic, we should take: watermelon, ice cream, and pie.

Junk Drawer–Exercise C

Identify and correct any misuse of parenthesis below. Not all sentences are incorrect.

1. The (whole) point is to catch lightning bugs.

2. I really want to talk to Tom (tonight).

3. Have you ever wondered (what it is) that makes rivers flow?

4. Road signs are a fundamental part of driving (even if they sometimes mess up the scenery).

5. It's time (right now) to take a stand.

Junk Drawer–Exercise D

Identify and correct any misuse of dashes below. Not all sentences are incorrect.

1. It's not advisable—to pursue dangerous relationships.

2. I think it's going to snow today—I really wish it wouldn't.

3. Refrigerate after opening—seriously.

4. The imagination—can't conceive a color—that doesn't exist.

5. Rainy weather can be—either soothing—or depressing.

Junk Drawer–Exercise E

Identify and correct any misuse of exclamation points below. Not all sentences are incorrect.

1. That's fantastic!!!!

2. Wow! You look really nice tonight.

3. You may think you're hungry, but chances are it's just thirst.

4. YouTube is a great place to learn new skills!!

5. What are you looking for?!

Junk Drawer–Exercise F

Identify and correct any misuse of question marks below. Not all sentences are incorrect.

1. This is a really important meeting for you, isn't it?

2. I think that tea should be served at five?

3. How are you doing?

4. I wonder what time the movie starts?

5. I'm not sure if this will work out?

Answer Key: Junk Drawer–Exercise A

1. I hope they arrive today; that would be wonderful. **(no change necessary)**

2. That picture is phenomenal, and it's the original.

3. I'd really like to visit Tokyo, Japan; Christchurch, New Zealand; and Johannesburg, South Africa.

4. Whenever I take a nap**,** I always feel great.

5. The meeting times are at 4:30, today; 5:30, tomorrow; and 6:30, Wednesday.

Answer Key: Junk Drawer–Exercise B

1. The ingredients I will use are carrots, parsnips, and nutmeg.

2. This is my favorite thing: sleeping in. **(no change necessary)**

3. Don't forget the following items: sunscreen, bug spray, and matches.

4. It's time to say sorry.

5. On our picnic, we should take watermelon, ice cream, and pie.

Answer Key: Junk Drawer–Exercise C

1. The whole point is to catch lightning bugs.
2. I really want to talk to Tom tonight.
3. Have you ever wondered what it is that makes rivers flow?
4. Road signs are a fundamental part of driving (even if they sometimes mess up the scenery). **(no change necessary)**
5. It's time (right now) to take a stand. **(no change necessary)**

Answer Key: Junk Drawer–Exercise D

1. It's not advisable to pursue dangerous relationships.
2. I think it's going to snow today. I really wish it wouldn't.
3. Refrigerate after opening—seriously. **(no change necessary)**
4. The imagination can't conceive a color that doesn't exist.
5. Rainy weather can be either soothing or depressing.

Answer Key: Junk Drawer–Exercise E

1. That's fantastic!
2. Wow! You look really nice tonight. **(no change necessary)**
3. You may think you're hungry, but chances are it's just thirst. **(no change necessary)**
4. YouTube is a great place to learn new skills.
5. What are you looking for?

Answer Key: Junk Drawer–Exercise F

1. This is a really important meeting for you, isn't it? **(no change necessary)**

2. I think that tea should be served at five.

3. How are you doing? **(no change necessary)**

4. I wonder what time the movie starts.

5. I'm not sure if this will work out.

Verb Power

Verbs act as the engine of the sentence. To strengthen your style, pay attention to the verbs you choose.

Avoid "to be" Verbs

Avoid overusing forms of the verb "to be," such as *is, are, was, were, am, being,* and *been.* These verbs do not convey action but act as a kind of equals sign, linking one part of the sentence to the next.

> You are a nice dresser.   You = a nice dresser.

When possible, choose to convey detail and action rather than indicate a state of being.

> Weak: The sun was really bright on the snow.

> Stronger: The sun shone brightly on the snow.

> Weak: Being a nice person is a good way to be happy. (Three forms of "be")

> Stronger: Kindness leads to happiness.

Avoid Passive Voice Constructions

Passive voice is a backward sentence that focuses too much on the recipient of an action rather than the doer of the action. To fix this problem, be clear about who is doing what. Determine what the real subject of the sentence is and what it is doing, then reword accordingly.

> Passive: The election's outcome was decided by the Supreme Court. (Who did the deciding? The Supreme Court.)

> Active: The Supreme Court decided the election's outcome.

> Passive: The suspect was being held in custody by the police. (What is the real

action in this sentence and who is doing it?)

Active: The police held the suspect in custody.

Passive: Accusations were made and feelings were hurt. (Who accused? Whose feelings were hurt?)

Active: The supervisor accused his coworkers and hurt their feelings.

Avoid unnecessary helping verbs

Helping verbs (forms of *be, have, can*—to name a few) perform a legitimate role, but they are often used unnecessarily. Notice how the second example in each pair is clean and to-the-point.

The day <u>had been</u> hot.

The day was hot.

We <u>had</u> worked all day and <u>had had</u> a good time.

We worked all day and had a good time.

She <u>had been being</u> rude all night.

She was rude all night.

Verb Power–Exercise A

The following student writing sample overuses forms of the verb "be." Rewrite the sentences using a stronger verb.

1. The snow was gentle as it fell to the earth and was like tiny winter kisses on my cheeks.

2. I was slow as I stepped through the blizzard on my way to do some Christmas shopping.

3. I stopped because I was distracted by the pretty red, green, and white gowns at the dress store that was large.

4. I wasn't daring enough to venture inside, but I enjoyed seeing dresses that were perfect and matched my holiday mood.

5. I was excited to reach the toyshop where I was hopeful I would find a present

that was perfect for my cousin.

6. Inside, contraptions, bells, and children were noisy.

7. I picked through the toys, which were delightful, until I found a pretty little doll that was blue eyed and a brunette.

8. I made my purchase and was gleeful as I left the store that was so enchanting.

9. Before I went home, I decided to warm up in the café which was nearby.

10. Sipping a cup of cocoa that was hot while watching the snow, which was nearly a foot high, outside the café window was a perfect end to my day.

Verb Power–Exercise B

Rewrite the following sentences to avoid passive voice construction.

1. A hard time was had by me when learning to play the piano when I was younger.

2. I was told by my mom to practice every day, but it was hated.

3. I was forced by her to sit down on the bench and run through my scales.

4. Playing scales was thought to be boring, and something more dramatic was wanted instead.

5. One day, a song called "Wild Horsemen" was discovered by me.

6. A lot of time was spent practicing it because it was exciting, and it was always played fast and loud.

7. It was found that the more my scales were practiced, the better I got at playing fast.

8. It must've been known by my mom that practicing scales would lead to good things.

9. Except, after a while, "Wild Horsemen" was played so much that she started to be annoyed.

10. I was asked to find a new song, but it was the only song that was known by me.

Verb Power–Exercise C

Rewrite the following sentences to eliminate unnecessary helping verbs. (Sometimes helping verbs are just fine. For this exercise, assume they are unnecessary.)

1. There have been many new and upcoming genres in the world of young adult literature.

2. One of the genres that has been having an impact is that of the dystopian novel.

3. Dystopia can be described as a broken and tyrannical society that could have been post apocalyptic.

4. There have been many different types of dystopian novels.

5. One type has been a lower class protagonist who has been having rebellious notions and goes against the restraints of the government.

6. Another type can be a protagonist from the upper class who might have been doubting the current way of life.

7. Many dystopian novels have been having a lot of violence.

8. Sometimes, the violence has been necessary to reveal the evils that societies can be having.

9. Some dystopian novels have not been ending happily.

10. But the best ones have been the ones that can have happy and hopeful endings.

Answer Key: Verb Power–Exercise A

Answers may vary.

1. The snow gently fell to the earth and caressed my cheek like tiny winter kisses.

2. I stepped slowly through the blizzard as I headed toward Main Street to do some Christmas shopping.

3. I stopped, distracted by the pretty red, green, and white gowns at the large dress store.

4. I didn't dare venture inside, but I enjoyed seeing the perfect dresses that matched my holiday mood.

5. I filled with anticipation as I reached the toyshop where I hoped I would find the perfect present for my cousin.

6. Inside, contraptions whirred, bells rung, and children giggled.

7. I picked through the delightful toys until I found a pretty little doll with blue eyes and brown hair.

8. I made my purchase and gleefully left the enchanting store.

9. Before I went home, I decided to warm up in the local café.

10. Sipping a cup of hot cocoa while watching the snow gather outside the café window perfectly completed my day.

Answer Key: Verb Power–Exercise B

Answers may vary.

1. I had a hard time learning to play the piano when I was younger.

2. My mom told me to practice every day, but I hated it.

3. She forced me to sit down on the bench and run through my scales.

4. I thought playing scales was boring, and I wanted to play something more dramatic instead.

5. One day, I discovered a song called "Wild Horsemen."

6. I spent a lot of time practicing it because it was so exciting, and I always played it fast and loud.

7. I found that the more I practiced my scales, the better I got at playing fast.

8. My mom must've known that practicing scales would lead to good things.

9. Except, after a while, I played "Wild Horsemen" so much that it started annoying her.

10. She asked me to find a new song, but it was the only song I knew how to play.

Answer Key: Verb Power–Exercise C

Answers may vary.

1. There are many new and upcoming genres in the world of young adult literature.

2. One of these impactful genres is the dystopian novel.

3. Dystopia indicates a broken and tyrannical society that is post apocalyptic.

4. There are many different types of dystopian novels.

5. One type shows a lower class protagonist who has rebellious notions and goes against the restraints of the government.

6. Another type shows a protagonist from the upper class who doubts the current way of life.

7. Many dystopian novels display a lot of violence.

8. Sometimes, the violence is necessary to reveal the evils of society.

9. Some dystopian novels don't end happily.

10. But the best ones are the ones that have happy and hopeful endings.

Sentence Variety

Good writing contains sentences of a diverse lengths and grammatical structures. This helps give writing a sense of rhythm and variety.

Vary Sentence Structure

Avoid repeating the same construction too often within a paragraph by combining a variety of sentence patterns. In the following example, the writer gets into a rut of starting too many sentences with dependent clauses.

> While I enjoy skiing, I like snowboarding as well. Although fresh powder is best for snowboarding, well-groomed slopes are best for skiing. Since I can't do both, I have to choose which one I will do. Before I hit the slopes, I check to see how much it snowed the night before.

There are many ways to increase sentence variety, but notice how a mixture of sentence structures makes the paragraph less tiresome to read.

> I enjoy skiing and snowboarding. They're really different though. Fresh powder is best for snowboarding, but well-groomed slopes are great for skiing. Unfortunately, that means I have to choose between them. Before I hit the slopes, I check to see how much it snowed. The conditions make all the difference.

Vary Sentence Length

Too many short, simple sentences make writing sound childish. Too many long, complex sentences wear on the reader's attention. Varying the length and complexity of your sentences helps provide rhythm and interest in your paragraphs. In the following example, notice how the short sentence, "I agree," provides a break after the more complex sentence before.

> Smith makes the argument that while our civil liberties must be protected from the encroachment of a security state, we cannot become so paranoid

about government power that we ignore the very real and preventable threats of terrorism. I agree. Surely we can find a balance between liberty and security without going to extremes.

Complex sentences can add interest to your writing, but some sentences just seem very long and cumbersome, stringing together one clause after another. It is best to simply break these long and rambling sentences into smaller, more manageable sentences.

> Rambling: They were going to have a picnic, but it started to rain, so everyone decided to go to a restaurant on the other side of town that had lots of space for big families even though some people in the group just wanted to wait and see if it would stop raining. (one sentence)

> Better: They were going to have a picnic, but it started to rain. Everyone decided to go to a restaurant on the other side of town with space for big families. Some in the group, however, wanted to wait and see if it would stop raining. (three sentences)

Sentence Variety–Exercise A

In the following paragraph, every sentence uses the same construction. Add sentence variety to the paragraph to make it more interesting to read.

> Many people have a phobia, and they can sometimes be debilitating. Some phobias do not stop people living normally, and they can go on living their lives without it affecting them. The number one phobia is of public speaking, and it is not something most people have to do on a daily basis. Another phobia involves a fear of getting sick, and this can make a person not want to leave their house. Phobias can sometimes seem humorous, and one of those phobias is that of clowns. Clowns are often innocent and charming, and they are also used as disturbing murderers in horror movies. Sometimes it is not known where a phobia comes from, and childhood traumas can usually play a part. A well-trained psychiatrist can usually help those who suffer from phobias, and people can get back to living a normal, fear free, life.

Sentence Variety–Exercise B

In the following paragraph, there are too many short sentences. Combine some of the sentences to add variety to the sentence length.

> I have a problem. I stay up late reading. I always have to wake up early. My work starts at seven. It makes me very tired. I just can't put a good book down. I'll get

to a good part. I'll look at the clock. It will be midnight. I tell myself, "One more page." I always read at least fifty. I decided to read boring books instead. I thought they would put me to sleep. Instead, I'm just bored. That didn't work. I have a new plan, though. I will get a later shift. That might not work. If it doesn't, I'll quit. I know of the perfect job. I'll apply to be a nightshift tollbooth attendant. I will be able to read late. I will also be working. What could be better?

Answer Key: Sentence Variety–Exercise A

Answers may vary.

Many people have a phobia, which can sometimes be debilitating. On the other hand, some phobias do not stop people living normally, and they can go on living their lives. The number one phobia, for example, is of public speaking. The good news is, public speaking is not something most people have to do on a daily basis. Another phobia involves a fear of getting sick. Unfortunately, this can make a person not want to leave their house. However, phobias can sometimes seem humorous, such as the fear of clowns. Clowns are often innocent and charming. But, in many cases, they are also used as disturbing murderers in horror movies. Sometimes it is not known where a phobia comes from, but childhood traumas can usually play a part. In most cases, a well-trained psychiatrist can usually help those who suffer from phobias so that people can get back to living a normal, fear free, life.

Answer Key: Sentence Variety–Exercise B

Answers may vary.

I have a problem. I stay up late reading, but I always have to wake up early because my work starts at seven. It makes me very tired. I just can't put a good book down! As soon as I get to a good part, I'll look at the clock (usually it's midnight) and tell myself, "One more page." I always read at least fifty. However, the other day, I decided to read boring books. I thought they would put me to sleep. Instead, I'm just bored. Since that didn't work, I have a new plan. I will get a later shift, and if that doesn't work, I'll quit because I know of the perfect job. I'll apply to be a nightshift tollbooth attendant, which will allow me to read late while I'm working. What could be better?

Awkward Sentences

Sometimes a sentence just doesn't sound right because it has a confusing and awkward structure. If you find yourself slowing down or stumbling over a certain sentence while reading aloud, you might need to rewrite the sentence and phrase it more clearly.

How to Fix Awkward Constructions

There is no single rule or technique to correct awkward phrasing. A writer must develop an "ear" for what sounds right and be willing to reword a sentence until it sounds smooth, clear, and direct. Sometimes the act of writing can overcomplicate what we want to say. With this in mind, pretend to describe your writing subject to a close friend. Notice how clear it sounds when simplified. Say it aloud, and then write it down. This is often a great fix for awkward sentences.

> Awkward: Taking life a day at a time is how I think it should be done to be happy.

> Better: Taking life one day at a time will make you happy.

A more methodical approach to fix an awkward sentence is to identify subject and verb, then cut the sentence down accordingly. Ask yourself, "What is this sentence about—what is the core subject?" (Choose a noun.) Then ask, "What is this subject doing?" (Choose a verb.) Try to choose a strong verb that conveys action, not a "be" verb.

> Awkward: The fact that we don't eat a balanced diet is our biggest health problem and that we don't get enough exercise is also a big issue.

What is this sentence about? At first it seems it is about a bad diet, but then another important subject is tagged on the end—not enough exercise. So the sentence is about **poor diet and lack of exercise** (subject). What do these things do? We don't just want to say they "are" an issue. "Are" does not convey action. What do poor diet and lack of exercise do? They **contribute to** or **result in** or **cause** (possible verbs) our greatest health problems.

> Better: Poor diet and lack of exercise contribute to our greatest health problems.

Here's another example.

Awkward: The article sums it up pretty well regarding what her plan is about.

What is this sentence about? **The article** (noun). What does the article do? (Notice the question doesn't ask for a weak verb—what the article "is.") It "**sums up**" her plan. Is there a better verb than "sums up"? What about **summarizes**? What else do articles do? They **present** information (possible verbs).

Better: The article summarizes her plan well.

Also: The article presents an effective summary of her plan.

Avoid Word and Phrase Repetition

Sometimes writers latch onto a nice word or phrase and then wear it out. Two repeat offenders appear in this short paragraph: "successful implementation" and "democracy/democratic."

America was the first country to **successfully implement** a **democracy** guaranteed by a constitution. The process was not easy and involved a lot of debate among the Founding Fathers, but eventually they were able to **successfully implement democratic** elections. The **successful implementation** of the Bill of Rights eventually brought reluctant colonies into the new **democracy**.

Instead, consider using synonyms (different words, same meaning) or simply a fresh approach to the same concept. Notice how the word "successful" is not used below; instead, the success is evident. Effective word choices essentially speak for themselves.

America was the first country to **implement** a **democracy** guaranteed by a constitution. The process was not easy and involved a lot of debate between the Founding Fathers, but eventually they were able to hold **democratic** elections. Passing the Bill of Rights eventually brought reluctant colonies into the new nation.

Avoid Clichés

Clichés are overused phrases that have become predictable and dull. When people read, they want to hear new and fresh language that provides an original point of view. Here are just a few examples of the many clichés.

Clichés are a dime a dozen.

Her words cut like a knife.

Beauty is skin deep.

I couldn't believe my eyes.

The room was as dark as a cave.

What goes around comes around.

Seeing is believing.

Avoid blind dates like the plague.

Avoid Excessive Intensifiers and Qualifiers

Intensifiers are words that attempt to add force or weight to a sentence, or "intensify" it. If these words are used too often, they can actually weaken and water-down the writing.

It is **really** amazing how intensifiers make sentences **very** cumbersome.

I am **so** glad I know how to avoid making this **extreme** mistake **so** often.

Qualifiers are words that indicate the limits of your claim. They are often appropriate and necessary, but too many make your writing sound wishy-washy.

Gun laws are **probably** a good idea **most of the time.**

Occasionally torture **might** be necessary **in some cases.**

For the most part it has been a **somewhat** good year.

Awkward Sentences–Exercise A

Identify and correct any awkward constructions in the following student sample. Not all sentences are incorrect.

1. Deciding what pajamas to wear is a tricky business.

2. You have to determine the first thing, which is how warm you want to feel that night.

3. That determines whether you are wearing sweats or shorts, or it determines if you'll wear fleece or silk.

4. Then what kind of mood you're in is what you have to decide.

5. For instance, do you want to wear polka-dots, or maybe you want to wear stripes?

6. Looseness, that is also a question of consideration.

7. Sometimes you want something clingy, others, baggy.

8. Once you've decided on all that, there are usually a few options left.

9. A whim is usually the narrowing down factor for that.

10. Then, you are at last prepared to slip into the perfect pair of pajamas.

Awkward Sentences–Exercise B

The sentences below are a clichés; find a more original way to say each.

1. We're reinventing the wheel.

2. That's so by the book.

3. Just sweep it under the rug.

4. Shape up or ship out!

5. This has gone to pot.

6. It's crunch time.

7. The more the merrier.

8. If you can't beat 'em, join 'em.

9. He chewed me out.

10. Beggars can't be choosers.

Awkward Sentences–Exercise C

Identify and correct any excessive intensifiers or qualifiers below. Not all answers are incorrect.

1. I sometimes wonder why people often whine.

2. It's probably not a big deal at all.

3. It's really, really cool that he actually did that for you!

4. Sidewalk chalk is kind of a fun activity sometimes.

5. I really can't believe summer is over already.

6. It's occasionally unclear how very much you love me.

7. How incredibly helpful that airports have plug in booths.

8. I really, really, really like that movie!

9. I guess I could maybe go out with you sometime.

10. Honestly, that is hardly a need.

Answer Key: Awkward Sentences–Exercise A

Answers may vary.

1. Deciding what pajamas to wear is a tricky business. **(no change necessary)**

2. First, you have to determine how warm you want to feel that night.

3. That determines if you're wearing sweats, shorts, fleece, or silk.

4. Then you have to decide what kind of mood you're in.

5. For instance, do you want to wear polka-dots or stripes?

6. There is also the question of looseness.

7. Sometimes you want something clingy and sometimes you want something baggy.

8. Once you've decided on all that, there are usually a few options left. **(no change necessary)**

9. That selection is usually narrowed down on a whim.

10. Then, you are at last prepared to slip into the perfect pair of pajamas. **(no change necessary)**

Answer Key: Awkward Sentences–Exercise B

No suggestions provided as answers may vary depending on context.

Answer Key: Awkward Sentences–Exercise C

1. I ~~sometimes~~ wonder why people often whine.

2. It's probably not a big deal ~~at all~~.

3. It's ~~so,~~ really cool that he **~~actually did~~** that for you!

4. Sidewalk chalk is **~~kind of~~** a fun activity.

5. I really can't believe summer is over already. **(no change necessary)**

6. It's unclear how ~~very~~ much you love me.

7. How incredibly helpful that airports have plug in booths. **(no change necessary)**

8. I really **~~really, really~~** like that movie!

9. ~~I guess~~ I could **~~maybe~~** go out with you sometime.

10. Honestly, that is hardly a need. **(no change necessary)**

Wordy Sentences

Wordy sentences contain many *unnecessary* words. These sentences feel "watered down"—like you have to do a lot of work to gain a little information. Good writing is dense and concise; the words in the sentence work hard. Consider the following revisions.

Wordy: A few inches of snow **on the ground is all that** is necessary **in order for a person to be able** to go sledding. (bolded words could be cut)

Better: Sledding requires only a few inches of snow. (all hard-working words)

Wordy: **All of the** students **who are** new **to this school** are required to attend a meeting **that has been scheduled for** Friday **the** 22**nd of** September. (bolded words could be cut)

Better: New students are required to attend a meeting on Friday, September 22.

The problem with wordiness *is not about the quantity of words*; there is nothing wrong with a sentence having 25 or even 75 words as long as those words add information and detail. When reducing wordiness, be careful not to kill the richness and expressiveness of your writing.

Not wordy: A bird with crimson wings glided from the jungle canopy and landed gracefully on a nearby rock.

Not better: A bird flew from the trees to a rock.

Phrases and Constructions to Avoid

Wordy: **It was** George Washington **who once said**, "Happiness and moral duty are inseparably connected."

Better: George Washington **said** "Happiness and moral duty are inseparably connected."

Wordy: **Due to the fact** that class is cancelled, we will postpone the quiz.

Better: **Because** class is cancelled, we will postpone the quiz.

Wordy: **In spite of the fact** that I am failing, I have enjoyed the class.

Better: **Although** I am failing, I have enjoyed the class.

Wordy: I bought a dog for **the purpose of providing me with** companionship.

Better: I bought a dog **for** companionship.

Wordy: I will return your papers **in the near future.**

Better: I will return your papers **soon.**

Wordy: **In my own personal opinion** torture is always wrong.

Better: **In my opinion** torture is always wrong.

Also: Torture is always wrong.

Note: Sometimes wordiness results from a desire to cheaply meet the minimum word requirement of a writing assignment. Most instructors prefer concisely worded writing even if it comes up a little short.

Wordy Sentences–Exercise A

Identify the wordy sentences in the following list, and then reword them accordingly. Not all sentences are wordy.

1. It was just the other day when I got a new typewriter.

2. I know that computers are a lot more efficient, but I love it.

3. The typewriter is one of those classic models that they used to have back in the old days.

4. The fact is, I keep on feeding all my spare scraps of paper and stuff through it.

5. And it really doesn't even matter what I end up typing.

6. I could type anything at all, and I imagine it would still be satisfying.

7. The problem is that the ink has started to imprint lighter and lighter.

8. It's very clearly shown that it is in fact running out of ink.

9. I don't really have an idea of what I'll end up doing after that.

10. I seriously have no idea how I would be able to change an ink cartridge on one of these things!

Wordy Sentences–Exercise B

Identify the wordy sentences in the following student sample, and then reword them accordingly. Not all sentences are wordy.

1. I just have to say that I have the coolest husband in the entire world.

2. It was just the other day when he had a Hogwarts acceptance letter dropped off for me at my work.

3. The next morning after that, over breakfast, he had me go online so that I could take this Sorting Hat quiz thing.

4. Because of all that, I decided to wear Ravenclaw colors that day because that's the group I was sorted into.

5. Then, before I left for work, he used a huge sheet of white plastic to turn the front door into a wall.

6. It was very obvious to me and to everyone else that it was most definitely Platform 9 ¾.

7. To top it off, he gave me a box of Bertie Bots Every Flavored Beans for the road—since I missed the cart lady.

8. What happened next is he gave me a sort of schedule that basically turned all of my college classes into magic classes because he used ideas from the book.

9. For instance, I had "Major Authors of the Muggle World" and "Potions." You can imagine how that livened things up.

10. I guess what I am trying to say overall is that he's a real catch, even though this whole scenario inadvertently says that he has a witch for a wife.

Wordy Sentences–Exercise C

Rewrite the paragraph below to reduce wordiness without losing information or detail.

The essay that I chose to read for this assignment is called "Shooting an Elephant" and it was written by George Orwell. The essay is basically about how the author had to shoot an elephant that had gone on a rampage and killed a man. A lot of things happen in the story but the main point is that the author didn't really want to shoot the elephant, but he felt like he had to so that he wouldn't look foolish or cowardly in front of all the other people. The main thing that is interesting about this particular essay is how Orwell says that even though as a British police officer he was supposedly the one with the power, it was actually the crowd of people who were the ones that were controlling him. (135 words)

Answer Key: Wordy Sentences–Exercise A

Answers may vary.

1. I got a new typewriter the other day.

2. I know that computers are a lot more efficient, but I love it. **(not wordy)**

3. It's one of those old fashioned typewriters.

4. I keep feeding all my spare scraps of paper through it.

5. It doesn't matter what I type.

6. I could type anything, and it would still be satisfying.

7. The problem is that the ink has started to imprint lighter and lighter. **(not wordy)**

8. It's clearly running out of ink.

9. I don't know what I'll do after that.

10. I have no idea how to change an ink cartridge on one of these things!

Answer Key: Wordy Sentences–Exercise B

Answers may vary.

1. I have the coolest husband in the world.

2. Just the other day, he had a Hogwarts acceptance letter dropped off at my work.

3. The next morning over breakfast, he had me take a Sorting Hat Quiz online.

4. Consequently, I wore Ravenclaw colors that day.

5. Then, before I left for work, he used a huge sheet of white plastic to turn the front door into a wall. **(not wordy)**

6. It was most definitely Platform 9 ¾.

7. To top it off, he gave me a box of Bertie Bots Every Flavored Beans for the road since I missed the cart lady. **(not wordy)**

8. Next, he gave me a schedule that renamed all my classes using ideas from the book.

9. For instance, I had Major Authors of the Muggle World and Potions. You can imagine how that livened things up. **(not wordy)**

10. He's a real catch, even though this suggests he has a witch for a wife.

Answer Key: Wordy Sentences–Exercise C

Answers may vary.

In the essay "Shooting an Elephant," George Orwell relates a story in which he shoots an elephant that had killed a man during a rampage. Throughout the essay, Orwell admits that he didn't want to shoot the elephant but did it to avoid looking foolish or cowardly. Orwell, who was a British police officer at the time of the incident, writes that although he was the one with power, he felt compelled to carry out the expectations of the crowd. (80 words)

Quotations

Direct Quotations

Use quotation marks to indicate the exact language of a speaker or writer.

> Benjamin Franklin once said, "Any fool can criticize, condemn, and complain—and most fools do."

Do not use quotation marks for indirect quotations or paraphrasing (restating it in your own words).

> Benjamin Franklin said that most fools tend to criticize and condemn others.

Dialogue

When indicating dialogue between two or more individuals, create a new paragraph each time the speaker changes. (Go to a new line and indent.)

> "Why is it such a big deal?" said John. Jenny looked hurt. She had been looking forward to this trip for a long time.

> "It's a big deal to me," she said.

> "Let's talk about this tomorrow."

> They didn't discuss it again.

Generally, the first letter in a quotation is capitalized. However, if the quotation is a continuation of your sentence, it should be used without capitalization. Also, if the quotation is interrupted and then continued, there is no need to capitalize the second part.

> Smith argues that "the end of global hunger is in sight."

> "Can you imagine," Sue said, "that happening in front of dad?"

Quotations within quotations

Use single quotation marks to indicate a quotation within a quotation.

> Mark said, "My teacher told me that Ben Franklin once said 'Any fool can criticize, condemn, and complain.' I wonder if he was trying to drop a hint."

Uncommon or colloquial expressions

Quotation marks sometimes indicate a word or phrase that someone else uses, not what the author would normally use.

> My daughter gave me a handful of weeds and told me to put these "flowers" in water so they wouldn't die.

Titles of Short Works

Place quotation marks around the titles of short works such as poems, short stories, articles, songs, and TV programs.

> In English 101 we read George Orwell's "Shooting an Elephant."

> I find the story "A Rose for Emily" quite disturbing.

> We sang "America the Beautiful" at the parade.

Quotation Marks with Other Punctuation

Place commas and periods inside the quotation marks.

> "I can't accept your apology," she said.

> Einstein once said that "Imagination is more important than knowledge." This idea has comforted artsy slackers for years.

Question marks and exclamation points are placed inside the quotation marks if the question or exclamation is part of the original quote. If not part of the original quote, they are placed outside the quotation marks.

> He looked at me and said, "Do you have a problem?"

> Can you believe Einstein said "Imagination is more important than knowledge"?

Integrating Quotations

In academic writing, never plop a quotation in the middle of your writing without properly introducing it and then following it with further commentary or explanation.

Notice how the correct version sets up the context for the quote, introduces the author, and then follows the quote with additional, related commentary.

> Incorrect: In this paper I will explore attitudes toward nature in ancient times. "Forty-four of the sixty-six meanings of nature listed by Arthur Lovejoy and George Boas were already current in classical times" (Coates 23). Ancient Greeks and Romans had a sophisticated concept of the meaning of nature.

> Better: The idea of nature was a complicated category in classical Greece and Rome, as it is today. In an impressive survey of Western attitudes toward nature, historian Peter Coates notes that "Forty-four of the sixty-six meanings of nature listed by Arthur Lovejoy and George Boas were already current in classical times" (23). Those definitions, however, had little to do with modern ideas of finding enjoyment in unspoiled wilderness.

The first time an author is mentioned, use the first and last names. After that, use the last name only.

- According to one researcher, John Smith, "___."
- Smith argues that "___."

When you are choosing a verb tense for your quotation introduction, remember that discussion of books and articles is in present tense (i.e. *Ophelia says* [not said]). When discussing historical events, use past tense (i.e. *Martin Luther King, Jr. said* [not says]). In all of your writing, make sure to be consistent in tense.

Tip: Avoid "connect the quotes" essays.

Some essays appear to be a string of extended quotations only loosely connected with original commentary or analysis. Avoid this mistake by only using quotations that directly support your argument and paraphrasing sources when possible. Most of the writing in even heavily researched papers should be original content from the writer.

Quotations—Exercise

Underline and correct mistakes in the sentences below. Not every sentence is incorrect.

1. Have you ever read the poem The Raven by Edgar Allen Poe?
2. I told my dad "that I was going to be later than usual."
3. Thomas Edison said, "The most certain way to succeed is always to try just one more time".

4. "The most certain way to succeed," writes Thomas Edison, "Is always to try just one more time."

5. "Where are we going?" I said. "I don't know," she replied. "You asked me out so it's your job to decide." "Well, how about miniature golf?" I asked.

6. My friend said, "Just remember what you told me yesterday: "Never give up."""

7. Anderson argues that "the decline of jungles around the world will affect the quality of our air."

8. The Cosby Show was one of the most successful sitcoms in television history.

9. About every ten minutes the kids would ask, "Are we there yet"?

10. My cousin wondered "why she was having such a bad day."

Quotations Exercise: Answer Key

Problem areas have been underlined and corrected.

1. Have you ever read the poem "The Raven" by Edgar Allen Poe?

2. I told my dad that I was going to be later than usual.

3. Thomas Edison said, "The most certain way to succeed is always to try just one more time."

4. "The most certain way to succeed," writes Thomas Edison, "is always to try just one more time."

5. "Where are we going?" I said.
"I don't know," she replied. "You asked me out so it's your job to decide."
"Well, how about miniature golf?" I asked.

6. My friend said, "Just remember what you told me yesterday: 'Never give up.'"

7. Anderson argues that "the decline of jungles around the world will affect the quality of our air." **(no change necessary)**

8. "The Cosby Sho<u>w</u>" was one of the most successful sitcoms in television history.

9. About every ten minutes the kids would ask, "Are we there ye<u>t?"</u>

10. My cousin wondered <u>w</u>hy she was having such a bad da<u>y.</u>

Made in the USA
San Bernardino, CA
28 May 2019